Southern Tradition and Regional Progress

... the South once took a great tradition and made it a hitching-post instead of a steppingstone.

—Dykeman and Stokely,
Neither Black nor White

SOUTHERN TRADITION
and
REGIONAL PROGRESS

BY

William H. Nicholls

Chapel Hill

THE UNIVERSITY OF NORTH CAROLINA PRESS

917.5
N 51 s

39828
Sept. 1960

To My Son
DAVID

in the hope that he may know
a better South because I lived,
as I have known a better South
because my father lived before me.

Preface

WHEN I was elected President of the Southern Economic Association late in 1958, I faced with considerable trepidation the necessity of choosing an appropriate and timely theme for my presidential address, which was scheduled for presentation at Jacksonville in November, 1959. With my personal background and professional interests, however, the problem proved to be much easier than I had anticipated. Having become increasingly aware of the conflict between important Southern traditions and Southern economic progress, I found that the subject of the present book naturally suggested itself. As I explored the matter more deeply, it became clear that neither the tolerance of my fellow Association members as a captive audience nor the generosity of the Association's managing editor in reserving scarce journal space was sufficient to permit me to encompass all I needed to say if I was to execute my self-appointed assignment satisfactorily. Hence, what began with the objective of being contained within an hour's lecture grew by leaps and bounds into the present book.

Needless to say, a book such as this does not spring full-blown out of a void. I have come by my interest in the present subject through a long evolutionary process. As a native Southerner I have always had not only a "feel" for the Southern tradition in which I was reared but a normal "patriotic" urge to help to promote the social and economic welfare of the Southern region. My professional training in economics at Harvard University gave me the tools by which I might better understand and analyze the economic problems of underdeveloped areas such as the South. My field of specialization, the economics of agriculture, made me more than normally aware of the interrelationships between the economic and noneconomic aspects of life, which are particularly important under predominantly rural conditions. Hence, I welcomed the subsequent opportunity for complementary graduate study in political science, sociology, history, social psychology, and public law when I served as a Post-Doctoral Fellow of the Social Science Research Council at the University of Chicago. Without this post-doctoral training in the other social sciences, I would certainly never have had the temerity as an economist to undertake the broader analysis I have chosen to attempt here.

Despite this background, I spent the first decade of my professional career at Iowa State College and the University of Chicago on research in agricultural economic problems which had little if any relationship to the Southern region. Therefore, when in 1948 Vanderbilt University offered me a position which would permit me to return to the South and specialize on research problems relating to Southern agriculture, I was delighted to accept. Since then, I have devoted a substantial part of my time to the study of the nature and causes of the South's widespread rural poverty. In this endeavor it soon became clear that the solution to the principal economic problems of the rural South lies primarily outside of agriculture and that, without substantial additional Southern industrial-urban development, these problems will remain largely unabated. I have therefore given increasing attention more recently to the interrelationships between the agricultural and nonagricultural sectors of the Southern economy within the broader framework of over-all regional economic development.

Preface

At Vanderbilt my most extensive research in agriculture and economic development, which was supported by a large grant from the Rockefeller Foundation, has been concerned with the effects of industrial-urban development upon agricultural productivity and income in the Upper East Tennessee Valley area. This research produced results which left little doubt that within this study area those counties which had enjoyed significant industrial-urban development had also succeeded in raising their farm output and farm income per worker substantially as compared with contiguous counties which had remained largely rural-agricultural. My colleague, Anthony M. Tang, found very similar results in his parallel research on a Georgia–South Carolina Piedmont area. While these favorable effects of industrial-urban development upon nearby agriculture could be explained almost wholly in economic terms, I found myself increasingly concerned with a different question: why had some Southern areas had substantial industrial-urban development and others little or none?

Specifically, I was puzzled as to why Upper East Tennessee—which was historically at a disadvantage compared to most other parts of the South in its economic resources—had outstripped so much of the South well before TVA in the impressive extent of its industrial-urban development. Upon further investigation, I was forced to turn to largely noneconomic factors, related to this area's markedly different cultural tradition, for a plausible explanation. I concluded that the outstanding economic progress of this area was in significant part the result of its failure to share with other Southern areas most of the principal tenets of Southern tradition. This speculation in turn suggested that in parts of the South where Southern tradition was stronger the impulse toward economic progress would inevitably be weaker. As a result, I was becoming increasingly aware of the possible conflicts between tradition and progress within the greater South.

This view was reinforced by my extensive foreign travels during the last decade. In firsthand observations of the agricultural areas of such economically underdeveloped countries as Brazil, Turkey, and

India, I found that the conflicts between tradition and progress are there for all to see. I saw how the noneconomic elements in age-old traditions constantly offer serious barriers to increased material well-being. In this broader perspective, I also saw more clearly than before that the same kinds of conflicts and problems exist in the American South as well, although in far lesser degree. With the recent revivification in the South of traditional race antagonisms as a result of the school-integration issue, I completely lost any residual belief that the South could successfully reconcile tradition and progress.

It has become my firm conviction that the South must choose between tradition and progress. To use a medical analogy, I believe that the Southern economy is basically in good health, but it has certain gangrenous appendages which must be amputated if the central body is to thrive and prosper. The surgical problem would be a simple one if the patient did not mistakenly insist—whether from ignorance, stubbornness, or vanity—that these mortified parts are essential to his very life. Hence, my principal task here is educational rather than surgical. That is, I shall try to demonstrate that these parts (tradition) are in fact both gangrenous and dispensable and that, if the South wants a vigorous and prosperous economic life, they must be sacrificed for the good (progress) of the whole.

To be sure, just as the doctor inevitably has a bias in favor of health, so do I as an economist have a bias which favors progress. As a consequence, I have by no means limited my professional activities to my research endeavors. Instead, through public lectures and testimony before Congressional committees, through a year on the staff of the President's Council of Economic Advisers, and through membership on the Agricultural Committee of the National Planning Association, I have carried my full share of the burden of putting social and economic knowledge into action. My ventures outside of the ivory towers of academia have not produced impressive practical fruits. But at least they have given a satisfying outlet for my strong interest in helping to revise public policies along lines which will facilitate and accelerate the South's economic progress. They have also given me the opportunity to learn at first hand how Southern people are thinking and how their tradition-oriented attitudes are interfering with regional economic progress.

In focusing my attention here on those aspects of Southern tradition—as reflected in the South's value system, its social and political structures, and its way of looking at social and intellectual issues—which I find are serious barriers to Southern economic development, I have had to extend myself far beyond the normal boundaries of the discipline of economics. Nonetheless, I have striven to make of this book as serious and scholarly a study as my own limitations of time and knowledge would permit. Insofar as possible, I have based my excursions into the subject matter of the other social sciences upon the expert knowledge of specialists in these fields. My indebtedness to the writings of C. Vann Woodward in history, of V. O. Key, Jr., in political science, and of Howard W. Odum in sociology, is particularly great. However, I have found it impossible to limit my sources to such renowned specialists—in part because my task requires the support of generalists instead and in part because the products of scholarly research of necessity lag too far behind the times to serve my somewhat topical needs here.

As to the generalists, the social sciences have long since lost that unity of knowledge which they once possessed. While the increasing division of labor in scholarship has undoubtedly sharply improved its quality and accuracy, the resulting fragmentation of knowledge has not been without its unhappy side as well. Academic generalists are still sorely needed, although their efforts to pull the pieces together are likely to be scorned if not roundly condemned (admittedly often on good grounds) by their more specialized colleagues. Hence, the task of social generalization has tended to fall into the hands of literary academicians and journalists who are bold enough to rush in where most social scientists fear to tread. While such men inevitably overstep the bounds of accurate specialized knowledge now and then, the best of them—Edwin Mims, the Vanderbilt Agrarians, the contributors to Louis D. Rubin, Jr., and James Jackson Kilpatrick's *The Lasting South*, W. J. Cash,

James McBride Dabbs, and Wilma Dykeman and James Stokely—
have made perceptive, insightful, and often basically sound gen-
eralizations which deserve both respect and praise, not only for the
boldness of their objectives but for even the substantial achievement
of these objectives. I am happy to acknowledge my dependence
upon their writings in much of what follows.

In meeting the problem of topicality, I have also found some of the
South's great journalists and editors indispensable. Close to the nerve
centers of current Southern public opinion, such men as Harry S.
Ashmore, Ralph McGill, Jonathan Daniels, and William T. Polk
deserve respect for their broad perspective and their general intelligence, erudition, and culture. I gladly pay them such respect.
Furthermore, I should acknowledge my appreciation to the Southern Regional Council, whose comprehensive and reliable compila-
tions of comment on racial matters in the monthly *New South* and
in occasional news releases have proved an invaluable source of
information about the current Southern scene.

In closing this acknowledgment of sources, I should perhaps explain one conspicuous omission of a recognized authority on my
present subject. I have at no point referred to the monumental work,
An American Dilemma (New York, 1944), by the popularly much-
maligned Swedish economist-sociologist, Gunnar Myrdal. While
I have no fundamental disagreement with either Myrdal's analysis
or his value premises, I have preferred to base my argument on the
even more perceptive insights of such native Southerners as Cash,
Dabbs, Woodward, Key, Odum, Ashmore, and McGill, the in-
timacy of whose knowledge of and experience in the South was
beyond debate. If Myrdal's work has any serious fault, it is because
he was too much the logician and too permeated with broader
western values to appreciate fully (as most Southern writers have)
what Ashmore has called "the Southerner's remarkable capacity for
unreality, which still enables him to hold out against the logic of
argument and of events."

I am also deeply indebted to many of my academic colleagues at
Vanderbilt University for the sympathy they have shown for my

Preface

broad objectives and for the hours of thoughtful comment, criticism, and tutoring which they have so generously given to me in order that my errors in their respective fields of knowledge might be reduced if not entirely eliminated. I should particularly like to thank Dewey W. Grantham, Herbert Weaver, and Emmett B. Fields of the Department of History; Avery Leiserson and Robert J. Harris of the Department of Political Science; Wayland J. Hayes of the Department of Sociology; and my fellow economists, Anthony M. Tang and Rudolph C. Blitz. Since all of these colleagues were unsparing in their efforts to help me to comprehend their specialties, all remaining errors should be attributed to my own ignorance, audacity, or stubbornness.

I should also like to acknowledge that the most loyal supporter of this book in its formative stages was Edwin Mims, Professor Emeritus of English at Vanderbilt University. Professor Mims died on September 15, 1959, at the age of eighty-seven. Vigorous in mind and passionately devoted to a progressive South to the very end, he had recently been engaged in writing a book which in some respects was apparently parallel to mine. If his final efforts fail to see the light of day posthumously, let it be recorded here that after reading the first draft of this manuscript he declared with unbridled enthusiasm, "This is *my* book!" I am happy and honored to have had so great a Southerner as Edwin Mims as the joint author, even vicariously, of my present work.

Finally, I should like to express my appreciation to the Rockefeller Foundation for its generous grant in support of the larger project of which this book is a part; to Mrs. Roberta G. Brandon and Mrs. Mary Ann Fletcher for efficient and ever-cheerful secretarial assistance; and to the University of North Carolina Press for friendly encouragement and elegant technical editing of my manuscript.

W.H.N.

Nashville, Tennessee
September 15, 1959

Acknowledgments

THE AUTHOR is very grateful to the publishers or copyright holders who granted him permission to reprint herein excerpts from the following copyrighted materials:

Herbert Agar and Allen Tate, editors, *Who Owns America?* Houghton Mifflin Company, Boston and New York, 1936. Copyright 1936 by Houghton Mifflin Company.

Harry S. Ashmore, *An Epitaph for Dixie*, W. W. Norton & Company, New York, 1957, 1958. Copyright 1957, 1958, by Harry S. Ashmore.

W. J. Cash, *The Mind of the South*, Doubleday & Company, Garden City, New York, 1956 (Doubleday Anchor Books). Copyright 1941 by Alfred A. Knopf, Inc.

James McBride Dabbs, *The Southern Heritage*, Alfred A. Knopf, Inc., New York, 1958 (Borzoi Book). Copyright 1958 by James McBride Dabbs.

Wilma Dykeman and James Stokely, *Neither Black nor White*, Rinehart & Company, New York and Toronto, 1957. Copyright 1957 by Wilma Dykeman and James Stokely.

V. O. Key, Jr., *Southern Politics in State and Nation*, Alfred A.

Acknowledgments

Knopf, Inc., New York, 1949 (Borzoi Book). Copyright 1949 by Alfred A. Knopf, Inc.

Edwin Mims, *The Advancing South*, Doubleday, Page, & Company, Garden City. N.Y., 1926. Copyright 1926 by Doubleday, Page & Company.

Charner M. Perry, editor, *The Philosophy of Democracy*, University of Chicago Press, Chicago, 1943. Copyright 1943 by the University of Chicago.

A. C. Pigou, *The Economics of Welfare*, Macmillan & Company, Ltd., London, and St. Martin's Press, Inc., New York, 1948. Copyright 1948 by St. Martin's Press, Inc.

William T. Polk, *Southern Accent: From Uncle Remus to Oak Ridge*, William Morrow and Company, New York, 1953. Copyright 1953 by William T. Polk.

Louis D. Rubin, Jr., and James Jackson Kilpatrick, editors, *The Lasting South: Fourteen Southerners Look at Their Home*, Henry Regnery Company, Chicago, 1957. Copyright 1957 by Henry Regnery Company.

Twelve Southerners, *I'll Take My Stand: The South and the Agrarian Tradition*, Harper & Brothers, New York and London, 1930. Copyright 1930 by Harper & Brothers.

C. Vann Woodward, *Origins of the New South 1877-1913*, Louisiana State University Press, Baton Rouge, 1951 (Vol. IX of Wendell Holmes Stephenson and E. Merton Coulter, editors, *A History of the South*). Copyright 1951 by Louisiana State University Press and the Littlefield Fund for Southern History, the University of Texas.

Contents

Contents

Southern Tradition and
Regional Progress

CHAPTER

1

WHITHER THE SOUTH?

Apothecary. My poverty, but not my will, consents.
Romeo. I pay thy poverty, and not thy will.

—Shakespeare, *Romeo and Juliet*

THE South has been poor for a century. Relative to the rest of the nation, it is still poor today. To be sure, the South has made considerable economic progress, but in doing so it has held with surprising tenacity to traditional values. In some degree, the South has been traditional because it was poor. At the same time, it has also remained poor in part because it was traditional. It is these interrelationships between Southern tradition and Southern poverty which will concern me here.

Defenders of Southern tradition have sometimes argued that, unlike Romeo's apothecary, the South could and should remain "poor but honest." They have also warned that if the South accepts offers of greater material well-being (Romeo's forty ducats), it will not only corrupt itself but will be condemned, along with the giver, to pointless self-destruction. On the other hand, critics of Southern tradition have denied that Southern poverty has necessarily precluded a measure of dishonesty. If Romeo's gold was "worse poison

I

to men's souls" than the apothecary's potion, he nonetheless saw that "famine is in thy cheeks, need and oppression starveth in thine eyes," and knew that the apothecary would never say nay. From this point of view, as a defense of poverty, Southern tradition has constituted a rationalization and a mythology. Thus, it has (in Lewis Mumford's colorful phrase) encouraged the South "continually [to] gaze with enamored eyes upon its own face, praising its warts and pimples as beauty marks." [1]

As an economist, I am not here interested in Southern tradition as such. However, as one who has devoted the last decade to scholarly investigations of the problems of Southern economic development, I have become very much aware of the extent to which certain peculiar noneconomic factors in the Southern tradition have offered formidable barriers to the material progress of the region and if ignored or unrevised will continue to bar progress.* I shall try in this book to identify those elements of Southern tradition which may be appropriately associated with Southern poverty and whose abandonment may be a prerequisite if the South is finally to put an end to its poverty. Before turning to this major objective, I must set the stage for my investigation and, since clashes between systems of values are inevitable in such an endeavor, make my own personal values explicit.

---

* Economists interested in economic development cannot avoid concerning themselves with noneconomic factors. Even in underdeveloped countries, economists have frequently made analyses and policy recommendations which have suffered because they have failed to take the noneconomic factors sufficiently into account. (Cf. my recent article, "Accommodating Economic Change in Underdeveloped Countries," *American Economic Review*, XLIX [May, 1959], 156-68.) Therefore, it is not surprising that in the underdeveloped South—where these barriers to economic progress are less extreme, hence less perceptible—economists and business leaders have too easily overlooked their importance.

Old South v. New South: The Perennial Battle

SOME seventy years ago Henry W. Grady made his famous lament that in burying one of her native sons, Georgia could provide only a minister and a hole in the ground. Today Georgia could undoubtedly dispatch its native son much more impressively in material terms. In the realm of the spirit, however, the native son might take a whirl or two in his grave if he knew that his minister might well be secretly harboring integrationist sentiments. If the material accoutrements of a decent burial today bear the label "Made in the South," so does the tradition which keeps our departed Georgian a Rebel to the grave. Thus do times change yet remain the same.

The struggle between Old South and New South is nothing new; it dates at least from early Reconstruction days. In fact, it is ironic that two great Southerners who shared a common family name should have personified so well the opposing forces of this struggle. Edwin Mims compares the two as follows:

> [Thomas Nelson Page] was distinctly a romantic, looking back upon a vanished age which for him had many of the characteristics of a golden age; [Walter Hines Page] was a critic, seeing with clear eyes the shortcomings of his people, and attacking with brave heart the barriers that hampered them in their struggle toward a more progressive life. One was a [Virginia] aristocrat, fully conscious of the charm and prestige of the aristocracy whose traditions he had inherited; the other was a [North Carolina] democrat, believing in the possibilities that lay in the training of the backward people of the South, for to him democracy was not simply a theory of government but a state of society in which all men might find the opportunity for the development of their distinctive talents.

Mims was not an unbiased observer. He not only favored Southern industrial development but hailed the "veritable war of liberation

3

... against the conservatism, the sensitiveness to criticism, the lack of freedom that have too long impeded Southern progress." [2] Thus, he firmly aligned himself with the critics of the Old South and the proponents of the New South—from Henry W. Grady, General Daniel Harvey Hill, and Walter Hines Page through Ellen Glasgow, Howard W. Odum, and Rupert B. Vance to W. J. Cash, Harry S. Ashmore, and James McBride Dabbs.

However, the essential accuracy of Mims's characterization of the traditionalist position can be clearly demonstrated from the writings of those most faithful to the Old South—from Thomas Nelson Page to and beyond the Vanderbilt Agrarians *—who left no doubt whatsoever as to where they stood. They were satisfied with developing nothing less than a positive defense (as their forebears had once done for slavery) of the Southern agrarian-aristocratic tradition in all of its aspects. To them the fundamental cause of the Civil War was, said Frank L. Owsley, the fact that "the North was commercial and industrial, and the South was agrarian. The fundamental and passionate ideal for which the South stood and fell was the ideal of an agrarian society." The Agrarians deplored this triumph of industrialism over agrarianism, and Donald Davidson added: "What was worse for the nation, [the South] lost the peace—first in the Reconstruction, second by temporarily conforming, under the leadership of men like Walter H. Page and Henry W. Grady, to 'new South' doctrines subversive of its native genius." Unlike the North, wrote John Crowe Ransom, "The South never conceded that the whole duty of man was to increase material production, or that the index to the degree of his culture was the volume of his material production." They rejected, therefore, the values of industrialism, which "is an insidious spirit, full of false promises and generally fatal to [tradition]." [3]

In view of the shallowness of Southern thinking of their times,

* Since the hard core of Vanderbilt's Agrarians was in the university's Department of English, of which Professor Mims was long chairman, his progressive views were probably the prime if unnamed target of his Agrarian colleagues.

4

the advocates of both New and Old South frequently showed great
courage in the vigor and forthrightness with which they expressed
their views. Since it took more courage in the South to be a rebel
than a Rebel, it was not uncommon for the proponents of the New
South to seek escape from a hostile environment by self-exile or even
suicide.* In recent decades, the fact of Southern industrial-urban
development has fortunately gradually reinforced the voices of the
New South and has at least reduced the region's intolerance of dis-
senters from Old South traditions. Nonetheless, I shall seek to
demonstrate that, insofar as the New South has made material progress, it has done so in spite of the strongly inhibiting social, political,
psychological, and philosophical elements in the Old South's cultural
heritage. I shall also argue that if the transition from the Old South
to the New South is to be completed, many of those still-strong
qualities of mind and spirit which have made the South distinctive
must largely disappear.

With such an immodest objective in mind, I shall find myself
compelled not only to invade the normal preserve of the other
social sciences but must even project myself further into the un-
certain realm of philosophy and ethics. My findings, as a result,
may too often appear to be impressionistic and subjective rather
than solid and scientific. If so, given the paramount importance of
the problem at hand, I shall not apologize; but I do hope that my
analysis, with all its faults, will make Southern economists and
business leaders more aware of the noneconomic barriers to Southern economic progress; that it will stimulate other social scientists
(not to mention humanists and philosophers) to bring to bear more

* As V. O. Key, Jr. (*Southern Politics in State and Nation* [New York,
1949], p. 664) has observed: "A depressingly high rate of self-destruction
prevails among those who ponder about the South and put down their reflections in books. A fatal frustration seems to come from the struggle to
find a way through the unfathomable maze formed by tradition, caste, race,
poverty." Cf. W. J. Cash's strangely prophetic eulogy of Clarence Cason,
whose suicide Cash attributed to fear of the fiercely hostile attitude which
Cason knew would result from his forthcoming book critical of the South—
Cash, *The Mind of the South* (New York, 1956), p. 327.

fully and effectively the insights of their particular disciplines upon these vital matters; and that it will help the intelligent Southern layman to perceive and to resolve in his own mind any inconsistencies between traditional values and the will to progress.

The Economist and the Problem of Values

HAVING no professional obligation to separate values from analysis, the Southern Agrarians usually minced no words in arguing that the South could not industrialize and urbanize without destroying distinctly Southern traditions which they valued above all else. They did not hesitate to argue that Southerners *ought to* reject material progress and hold fast to the old traditions. As a social *scientist*, I must exercise more self-discipline. I shall not be able, of course, to avoid making important value judgments. But, for this very reason, I am obligated to make explicit my own value premises, the most important of which may be stated as follows: (1) I *favor* the achievement of sufficient additional Southern economic progress to eliminate interregional differences in per capita real incomes; * (2) I *believe* that further industrial-urban development of the South not only is essential but that it inevitably means the destruction of many of the Southern traditions which my ancestors held dear; and, forced thereby to make a choice, (3) I *prefer* that the South seek further material progress even at the cost of abandoning these traditional values. Even so, as an economist, I cannot appropriately say that Southerners *ought to* want higher per capita real incomes or that they *ought not* to give the noneconomic elements of the Southern tradition a higher priority than material progress. Nor can I, as economist, say that those who would put the preser-

* Compare below, where I define "economic progress" as an increase in per capita real income (per capita material well-being).

6

vation of certain Southern traditions first are "wrong" and that I am "right," since we are here in the extra-scientific realm of philosophy and ethics. Instead, as economist, I must state my problem in the following terms: *if* a majority of Southerners (here my unrepressed bias in favor of democracy remains) want as their foremost objective to achieve higher per capita real incomes, what are the barriers to and the means of attaining this social end?

Some may ask, why be such a purist? Did not the Agrarians demand that means be found to help "the little agrarian community resist the Chamber of Commerce of its county seat" and "to stop the advances of industrialism, or even undo some of them"? [4] Would more than a tiny minority of Southerners still accept such romantic, nostalgic, and even utopian views today? Isn't it clear that the South's rapid economic progress of recent decades not only has further weakened the hold of tradition but has become the primary social goal of most Southerners?

In reply, I must admit that until recently any re-examination of Southern Agrarianism would have looked absurd. However, the current crisis surrounding school desegregation has revealed that although Southern tradition is in a decline, it is far from bereft of vigor. This educational controversy may represent either the death throes preparatory to Ashmore's "Epitaph for Dixie" or the renascence of the traditional Southern values which some latter-day sectionalists still demand. Lest we underestimate the strength of tradition, let us recall Edwin Mims's words of 1926. After hailing the South's "remarkable industrial development, [and] an even more important and significant intellectual renascence," Mims tempered his optimism with a comment that has a familiar ring today: "The stage seems all set for wonderful progress; the obstacles seem to be removed; and then something happens; there is a resurgence of the old reactionary spirit, policies, and ideas. And in some respects the South looks worse . . . than it has looked at any time within the last decade or more." [5] In any case, whether one views the South's current convulsions with hope or alarm, a diagnosis of the causes is vital to understanding why the South has lagged behind in eco-

7

nomic development and why its further progress is fraught with extra-economic impediments.

For this purpose, I find the Vanderbilt Agrarians more instructive than their more moderate successors.* It is easy to give the Agrarians a place of prominence greater than they deserve, since they were always a small voice, little heeded even in their own environs. However, because their views were both extreme and explicit, the members of the Vanderbilt group did place in bold relief important elements of the Southern tradition. Because they were more literate and articulate than most other Southerners of conservative persuasion, yet gave their emotions free rein, their views offer relatively faithful (if highly intellectualized) reflections of some of the more broadly held traditional values which interest us here. Hating the sociologist, though innocent of social science, they also offer an excellent example of "the Southerner's remarkable capacity for unreality, which still enables him to hold out against the logic of argument and of events." [6] Particularly were they unrealistic in choosing traditional values over material progress without considering the relative costs of the alternatives. While the social scientist cannot properly say which alternative Southerners should choose, it is within his special competence to indicate the nature and extent of the costs which Southerners must weigh if their choice is to be rational and well-informed.

Apparently seeking to broaden their appeal, the Vanderbilt Agrarians became even more unrealistic in implying, although infrequently, that the preservation of Southern tradition was not inconsistent with achieving at least a modicum of material well-being, but they carefully avoided saying for whom and for how many. In this more persuasive mood, John Crowe Ransom wrote: "The South must be industrialized—but to a certain extent only, in moderation. . . . it will be fatal if the South should conceive it as her duty to be regenerated and get her spirit reborn with a totally

---

* For example, the fourteen Southerners who contributed essays to Louis D. Rubin, Jr., and James Jackson Kilpatrick, editors, *The Lasting South* (Chicago, 1957).

different orientation toward life." * In this instance the Vanderbilt Agrarians were less offensive than some of their own successors or even their more recent antagonists. One repeatedly finds both of the latter groups saying in effect what Rubin recently wrote: "The South must find a way to control industrialism, to admit it only on the South's own terms." [7] The very lateness of the South's economic development offers a real opportunity to avoid some of the excesses of Northern industrial-urban growth; with proper foresight and planning, the South can still avoid them. But it is unrealistic to argue, as most lay writers (both conservative and progressive) have tended to do, that the South can have it both ways. The social scientist can appropriately insist that this is not possible, that fundamentally a choice (however painful and unpleasant) between the values of agrarianism and industrialism must be made.

What Is Progress?

BEFORE I turn to my analysis of the conflicts between tradition and progress, perhaps I should indicate briefly what I mean by

* Twelve Southerners, *I'll Take My Stand* (New York, 1930), p. 22. In what was in many ways a sequel to *I'll Take My Stand* (Herbert Agar and Allen Tate, editors, *Who Owns America?* [New York, 1936]), Ransom added with a touch of good humor (p. 190): "The Agrarians have been rather belabored . . . as denying bathtubs to the Southern rural population. But I believe that they are fully prepared to concede the bathtubs." In the later book, however, the Agrarians appear to have conceded much more. Whereas the earlier book had been full of uncritical praise of essentially aristocratic values, strongly smacking of the big-planter class, the later book presented a political program whose hero was explicitly the small yeoman farmer, the views of the Agrarians having meanwhile taken on strong overtones more congenial with the agrarian radicalism of the old Southern Populist Movement.

9

"progress." Here I am concerned with progress in its economic or material aspects. By "economic progress" I mean an increase in per capita real income or (what amounts to the same thing) an increase in per capita material well-being in terms of real goods and services. According to this definition, the South could make economic progress even though its rate fell below that of the rest of the nation. However, I consider satisfactory only a rate of Southern economic progress which is sufficiently high to bring the South's per capita material well-being up to a par with that of the non-South—that is, up to 100 percent of the non-South rather than 50 percent (1940) or the 68 percent of recent years. Since the rest of the national economy is not going to stand still, this means that the South's relative economic progress must continue to proceed at a rate well above that of other American regions if the South is finally to close the gap which has so long separated its level of material well-being from the higher national standard.

My concern with the material side of Southern life does not mean that I believe that rich men are necessarily good men. But neither do I believe that men who live in squalor and ignorance, as many Southerners have long done, have the open sesame to the good life. These are not, it should be emphasized, the South's urban whites, who already have per capita incomes nearly as high as those of urban whites outside of the South, once allowances for the South's lower urban costs of living have been made. Rather, they are the South's nonfarm Negro population and its farm families, both white and Negro, whose average incomes are only about one-half of those of the corresponding families elsewhere in the United States. Since the South's low-income problem is largely centered on its Negroes and rural people, it is these groups which policies to promote Southern economic progress must seek most to aid. These economic facts of life also suggest the particular Southern traditions which must come into question here if economic progress is to be the South's goal. Not all Southern traditions but primarily those traditions associated with race and rural life are therefore most relevant to the present analysis.

In general, I shall also equate economic progress with industrial-urban development. This is not because I believe that all manufacturing industries are desirable or that cities are without their own serious human problems. I do not like sweatshop industries or city slums. On the other hand, I am not blind to the emptiness and hopelessness of much of the South's rural life and to its widespread rural slums from which escape is even more difficult. For example, in 1949, of all American farm families with cash incomes from all sources of less than $1,000, the South accounted for 71 percent. Unlike those in the rest of the nation, the South's low-income farm families included relatively few who were aged, disabled, widowed, or divorced. Rather, they consisted primarily of complete farm-operator families whose heads were male, able-bodied, and in their more productive years. Economists generally have agreed that such farm families were poor primarily because they produced little. They produced little because they lacked enough land and capital to make adequate farm incomes and at the same time they lacked off-farm job opportunities by which their meager farm incomes might be adequately supplemented.

My definition of economic progress does not of itself necessitate industrial-urban development. *If* there were a rate of outmigration from the South's low-income rural areas sufficient to reduce its farm population drastically and *if* additional farm capital sufficient to raise its productivity substantially were made available to Southern agriculture from outside sources, the South might be able to increase its per capita real income at a satisfactory rate without any further industrial development. However, I believe that history has already proved that outmigration alone cannot solve the South's low-income rural problem and that, without further industrial-urban development, the income-depressing effects of Southern agriculture's excess human population and deficit of farm capital cannot be fully corrected.

Because of the South's chronically overpopulated and low-income agriculture, large-scale outmigration is nothing new to the region. The older parts of the Southeast have peopled other regions continuously for more than a century.* In earlier days, Southern people moved in large numbers to better agricultural opportunities in the Midwest and, more recently, to expanding industrial opportunities in the North and West. Without the "safety valve" of outmigration, the rural South's economic problem would have been even more severe. Unlike the rural Great Plains, however, the South has had few low-income rural areas whose rates of outmigration, though high, were sufficient to result in adequate farm incomes for those families who remained behind. Instead, the rural South's high birth rates have usually filled its human reservoir more rapidly than it was being emptied by migration; the region has suffered a steady net drain on its limited public investment in the education and health of its youth as they left the community upon reaching their productive years; the pressure of population on the supply of land has kept Southern farm land values unduly high; and outside capital has failed to move into the low-income community.

The persistence of the South's position as a low-income region has made absolutely clear that moving people out will rarely solve the local economic problem unless, at the same time, sufficient farm capital and managerial assistance also move in.† In Southern rural areas which fail to attract industry, even large-scale outmigration may lead to abandoned farm land, social disorganization, and selective deterioration of the residual population unless additional farm capital is made available from outside sources. Such additional capital is absolutely vital if hopelessly uneconomic small farms are to

* During 1870-1950, the total population of twelve Southern states (excluding Delaware, Maryland, Texas, and Florida) increased more than threefold despite a total net outmigration of about 7,300,000 people, of whom 2,500,000 left during 1940-50 alone—compiled from Everett S. Lee, *et al., Population Redistribution and Economic Growth*, Vol. I (American Philosophical Society, *Memoirs*, XLV [Philadelphia, 1957]).

† In 1949, commercial farms in Central Iowa had three times as much capital per worker and more than three times as much net farm output per worker as in Tennessee. (Jackson V. McElveen and Kenneth L. Bachman, *Low Production Farms*, U.S. Dept. Agriculture, Agri. Info. Bulletin 108 [Washington, 1953], Tables 11-13.)

be consolidated into larger and more efficient family farms capable of developing successful livestock enterprises in combination with, or in lieu of, traditional crops and of using modern farm machinery economically.

Where a community's entire agriculture needs extensive reorganization—including such time-consuming improvements as building up pastures and livestock herds, fencing, and acquiring new buildings and equipment—great amounts of farm capital are required. Because livestock enterprises demand much greater managerial skills, more resources for training and assisting farm managers are also much needed. In most low-income Southern communities, farm capital and managerial assistance have not normally been forthcoming from either private or public sources. The farm credit and managerial skills which such communities can themselves provide have usually been both entirely inadequate and largely directed toward perpetuating the traditional low-income production patterns and practices rather than toward facilitating much-needed changes in the local agriculture.

Thus, my own reading of the economic history of the South indicates that the human and social costs of outmigration are great and that it is extremely difficult to achieve the combination of smaller farm population and larger farm capital and management resources needed to eliminate community-wide rural poverty. It is here that the South's historical lag in industrial-urban development emerges as a major factor accounting for its low-income farm problem.

Compared with other alternatives, industrial-urban development of rural areas greatly hastens the readjustments needed to achieve higher productivity and higher incomes for Southern agriculture,[8] for the following reasons:

(1) Because it is much easier to get underemployed farm people to change occupation without changing residence, local nonfarm job opportunities have a far more immediate and marked effect upon local incomes than do distant opportunities.

(2) The drain on local community capital (particularly public

investments in education, health, etc.) which accompanies out-migration is avoided.

(3) Industrialization usually involves the introduction from out-side of nonagricultural capital which increases local banking and credit resources and personal savings. Hence, local financial insti-tutions become more adequate for local credit needs, including those of the nearby agriculture. With rising local nonfarm wage rates, the community's farm operators are forced to find ways of using their own labor force more efficiently. At the same time, they can more easily find the capital and managerial assistance required for reorganizing their farm business on a higher productivity basis.

(4) With the growth of the local industrial-urban center, addi-tional nonfarm jobs are generated in the service industries. Thus, with new markets created for locally produced farm products, local business leadership has new incentives to improve farm marketing and processing facilities and to provide local farmers with the capi-tal and know-how needed to shift to new and more profitable lines of production.

(5) With improved local markets, nearby farmers are likely to enjoy the availability of a wider range of goods and services, pro-vided on a more efficient and competitive basis and with more ade-quate informational and credit facilities.

(6) With greater concentration of population and rising per capita incomes, such developing communities can supply much-improved public services, which will in turn raise nearby rural levels of living, improve the quality of agriculture's human re-sources, and stimulate still further economic development.

For such reasons, my own view is that an acceleration of indus-trial-urban development throughout the Southern region is vitally necessary to a solution of its problem of low-income rural areas. When I equate progress and industrialization in this book, I do so on the basis of a professional judgment derived from nearly a decade of economic research on the problems of Southern economic development and agriculture.

To sum up, it is my principal thesis here that the South's serious lag in per capita incomes is largely attributable to its insufficient rate of industrial-urban development and that the South's lag in industrial development is in substantial part the result of its stubborn adherence to a set of values inconsistent with a high rate of industrialization. So much said, I now turn to the heart of my analysis. What are the key elements in the distinctively Southern tradition, way of life, and state of mind which have hampered regional economic progress? The list is long but can be classified for convenience into five principal categories: (1) the persistence of agrarian values, (2) the rigidity of the social structure, (3) the undemocratic nature of the political structure, (4) the weakness of social responsibility, and (5) conformity of thought and behavior. In the next five chapters, I shall consider each of these matters in detail.

CHAPTER

2

THE PERSISTENCE OF
AGRARIAN VALUES

The agricultural population, says Cato, produces the bravest men, the most valiant soldiers, and a class of citizens the least given of all to evil designs.

—Pliny the Elder, *Natural History*

BECAUSE the South has been historically an agricultural region, it is only natural that its dominant value system has been agrarian in character. Certainly, it would be unreasonable to expect the South to have discarded the values of its agrarian tradition and to have replaced them with a new set of values—one perhaps totally alien and quite inappropriate to the existing order—in order to accommodate industrial development in advance. In today's more developed countries or regions, the triumph of the values that go with modern industrialism came gradually and was in effect an integral part of the transitional process from an agricultural to an industrial economy. In other words, the old agrarian values have usually died hard and then only as industrial-urban development built up irresistible forces against them. To attribute the South's low incomes (or lag in industrial development) to its agrarian values is in some degree question-begging and unrealistic. Within limits it would be more appropriate to argue that the South has persisted in its agrarian value system because of its lag in industrialization rather than to attribute the latter to its stubborn agrarianism.

However, even admitting that we face here another example of the perennial "hen and egg" problem, it is very important to try to understand why the Southern value system diverged so widely from the dominant national trend. Except for the South, all American regions experienced a process of almost continuous evolution in which agricultural and industrial progress went nearly hand in hand, with changes in the dominant value system never lagging very far behind. Why was the South different—permitting its agrarian value system to persist with only the most gradual modifications —and what have been the consequences?

The Old Southern Agrarianism: Progress Spurned

ACCORDING to a leading agricultural historian, "The early leadership of agriculture in America planted the seed of an intellectual tradition that in essence had two parts. The first of these was the idea of progress and scientific improvement. The second was the literary agrarianism derived originally from classical antiquity." As both a doer and a thinker, Thomas Jefferson personified both parts of this tradition. He was active in promoting scientific farming and devised what was possibly the first mathematical formula for a moldboard of least resistance for plows. At the same time, he established himself as the high priest of all future American agrarians by writing in the spirit of Cato and Pliny that "Those who labor in the earth are the chosen people of God"—a divine depository "for substantial and genuine virtue" and a firm rock against the corruption, subservience, venality, and unchecked ambitions of city folk.[1] Within Jefferson's own lifetime, however, forces were already under way which were ultimately to lead the South to lose interest in the idea of agricultural progress while embracing with increasing fervor the agrarian part of the early American tradition.

At a very early stage, Americans showed a mechanical inventiveness which was soon to make "Yankee ingenuity" an object of worldwide admiration. The spectacular development of labor-saving devices, which were welcomed in a new land faced with a scarcity of labor, not only formed the basis for both an industrial and an agricultural revolution in the United States but quickly raised the idea of indefinite technological progress into a generally accepted popular assumption. For most of American agriculture, the ultimate result was the triumph of commercial farming as a business over the agrarian ideal of farming as a way of life. Ironically, it was an early Yankee invention, the cotton gin, which caused Southern agriculture to take an opposite turn. By first making economically feasible the separation of short-staple lint from the seed, the cotton gin provided the foundation upon which the South's cotton economy was able to develop and prosper. The resulting phenomenal expansion of cotton production not only revived the moribund institution of slavery (the South's answer to the problem of labor shortage) but gave new life to the plantation system in Southern agriculture.[2]

The consequences of cotton, slavery, and plantation were not only the strengthening in the South of a relatively rigid, static, and oligarchical social and political structure (of which more later) but also the creation of attitudes unfavorable to technological progress even within agriculture. Its rejection of the idea of agricultural progress has been brilliantly analyzed by Dabbs: "The land and climate of the North was less suitable to slave labor than that of the South. Northerners, then, . . . set themselves to mechanical invention. From the rushing rivers they abstracted water power, and from the limited motions of the human body, eventually unlimited machine power. Thus, continually changing their way of making a living, they changed, and willingly, their society." The South, on the contrary, "always had a slight tendency to stop where it was; and—a fact of more importance—its machines, the slaves, were always eager to abet it in this tendency. . . . When the African had been reduced to manpower, there was little more you could do with him." In contrast, "the physical machines of the North were subject to indefinite improvement. . . ." [3]

While other Americans eagerly sought and promptly adopted new mechanical techniques and improved farming methods, Southern agriculture tended simply to repeat in the future what it had done in the past. To be sure, there were in the South occasional wealthy planters who interested themselves in prosecuting agricultural experiments—such as seed selection and plant breeding for better cotton varieties and livestock breeding for superior bloodlines—which led to agricultural improvements of a nonmechanical sort. But for the most part, the small but socio-politically dominant planter class—though increasingly involved in the intricacies of a commercial world economy—saw little need to share in the prevalent American idea of progress. So prosperous was cotton production in the ante-bellum period—thanks to its then very favorable terms of trade with England's and New England's manufactures and to the highly productive virgin soils of the Deep South—that the planter class could be wholly content with things as they were and could not yet see any disadvantages in the South's status as a colonial or tributary economy. Under these circumstances, most Southern planters found it both personally congenial and politically expedient to advocate an agrarian philosophy which positively opposed Southern industrial-urban development as an inferior way of life, as an unwanted carrier of the virus of Northern high-tariff sentiment, and as a threat to the solidarity needed to protect its supposedly vital interest in the institution of slavery.

But what of the much vaster numbers of middle-class yeoman farmers, particularly in the uplands of the South? Increasingly isolated economically and culturally from the mainstreams of American development, they persisted in a pioneer pattern of small-scale, largely subsistence farming which was far removed from the influences of national agricultural progress. While some of them did for a time enjoy temporarily favorable markets for grain and livestock, they soon lost them in competition with the newer, richer, and more level lands of the Midwest—a loss aided and abetted by the invention of the mechanical reaper by (for once) a Southerner, Cyrus McCormick, who became a commercial success only by removing his manufacturing operations from Virginia to Chicago. For more than a half-century thereafter, until tobacco became a major new cash crop, farmers outside the cotton belt failed to find significant alternative sources of cash income. The leaders of the upland areas of the South (notably East Tennessee) which lacked important staple cash crops suited to a slave system had decided long before the Civil War that their area's destiny lay in manufacturing rather than in agriculture. On the whole, they never accepted the dominant agrarian philosophy of the ante-bellum South but found it very difficult to make their voices heard in their planter-dominated state governments before the war.[4]

Given such an unsympathetic environment, few would-be industrialists arose from the South's own ranks and fewer from other regions found the South an attractive place to make their mark as manufacturers. At the same time, repelled by the low status of free labor in a slave society, Northern and foreign workers skilled in the manufacturing arts saw little advantage in migrating into the agrarian South. Thus, even before the disastrous effects of Civil War and Reconstruction, the South had developed a regional philosophy and social, political, and economic institutions which, despite the real but ephemeral agrarian prosperity of their own time, were unfavorable to the achievement of balanced and broadly based economic progress over a longer period.

The New South Movement: Progress Embraced

WAR and Reconstruction left the South generally impoverished. Completely stripped of their economic foundations, Southern planters were forced to turn to a system of crop-share wages for their Negro labor and of merchant credit at exorbitant interest rates for their working capital. As a result, the cotton belt was saddled with a low productivity organization of its agriculture from which it found escape almost impossible. Perhaps more important, the South stagnated when the rest of the nation was enjoying one of the most dynamic periods of its economic development. Under these dire circumstances, the gun barrels were hardly cold before prominent Southerners were vigorously voicing the opinion that the future of the South lay in an industrial order that would be the basis of a more enduring civilization. Such voices now found many sympathetic ears—in part because of the attribution of the South's military defeat to its lack of an industrial base, in part because of the belief that the Negro was unsuitable for anything but common farm labor, and in part because of the desperation with which many of the South's leading old families sought to get back on their feet. Many Southern states were soon busily engaged in a frenzied effort to attract industrial capital and skilled workers from the North and from abroad.

The most prominent voices in this New South movement were newspaper editors. One of the earliest and most influential spokesmen for the New South was "Marse Henry" Watterson of the Louisville *Courier-Journal*, who demanded a program of subsidies, tax exemptions, and privileged franchises to encourage the flow of Eastern capital into Kentucky. But it was largely from the seaboard states of Virginia, Georgia, and the Carolinas that the impulse toward industrialism and reconciliation spread over the South. The Anglo-Southerner and ex-Confederate editor of the Charleston

(S.C.) *News and Courier*, Francis W. Dawson, who began his campaign for Southern industry in the early seventies, did not hesitate to recommend to his adopted city "the importation of about five hundred Yankees of the right stripe [to] put a new face on affairs, and make the whole place throb with life and vivid force." Henry W. Grady of the Atlanta *Constitution* not only wielded his pen with widespread appeal but, as a powerful politician, brought Georgia under the control of its new industrialists and, as a famous orator, ranged far and wide in proclaiming the opportunities for investment in his region, the virtues of the self-made man, and the desirability of reconciliation with the Northeast. These editors and their business allies, wrote Vann Woodward, were not merely advocates of industrialism: "What is more important, they were preaching laissez-faire capitalism, freed of all traditional restraints, together with a new philosophy and way of life and a new scale of values." *

The New South's leaders were largely middle class in their origins and outlook. A large majority of the new captains of Southern industry were native-born but of nonslaveholding parents. While these industrialists usually found it politic to bring into their organizations men of authentic planter origin, whose names brought the prestige of aristocratic lineage or glorious war records, the latter seldom contributed much to the management and direction of the new firms. However, the old planter class and the new industrialists found much common ground in an economic conservatism which opposed incipient agricultural radicalism and expensive government. Spokesmen for the New South found it possible to sell their "bitter mixture of recantation and heresy" by identifying their cause with the downtrodden old South. According to Woodward, "along with the glittering vision of a 'metropolitan' and industrial

---

* C. Vann Woodward, *Origins of the New South 1877-1913* (Baton Rouge, La., 1951), pp. 6, 188, 146-48. Perhaps the ultimate in recantation took place when, in 1881, the Vicksburg *Herald* declared (quoted *ibid.*, p. 151): "We are in favor of the South, from the Potomac to the Rio Grande, being thoroughly and permanently Yankeeized."

South to come there developed a cult of archaism, a nostalgic vision of the past. One of the most significant inventions of the New South was the 'Old South'—a new idea in the eighties, and a legend of incalculable possibilities." [5] ✓

If the new industrialist class thus used the old planter class to gain its own ends—a coalition which successfully opposed the popular side of most economic and social issues—the actual extent of Southern industrialization during 1860-1900 was far from impressive. Chattanooga and, to a lesser degree, Knoxville became the budding new industrial centers of East Tennessee under the initial impetus of openly solicited "carpet-bagger" capital and management. Again, on the basis of Alabama and Nashville capital and entrepreneurship and an unusually favorable conjunction of natural resources, Birmingham was able to establish itself as a Southern Pittsburgh. A group of aggressive North Carolina entrepreneurs effectively built a tobacco-products empire, of which Richmond was a major capital. But the principal achievement of the industrialization movement was, of course, the establishment of the cotton-textile industry, with Atlanta a major beneficiary. Hundreds of cotton-mill villages came to dot the dreary landscape of the Piedmont. Unfortunately, as both Woodward and Cash have emphasized,[6] the social and economic organization of these mill villages represented the bodily transfer of the plantation system from cotton field to textile factory—a fact which did little to make industrialization a very attractive, democratic, or self-sustaining process.

While South Carolina and Georgia did gain on the nation as a whole in per capita value added by manufacture during 1860-1900, in 1900 they still stood at only 25 to 29 percent of the national average. In 1900, the population of the South as a whole was only 18 percent urban, and as late as 1920 more than 50 percent of Southerner workers were still engaged in agriculture. During 1870-1900, net outmigration from nine states of the Old Southeast amounted to some 1,300,000 people, 58 percent of them white.*

* During 1860-1900, South Carolina's per capita value added by manufacture increased from 18 to 25 percent of the national average; Georgia's from

Thus the rate of industrialization in the South during the post-bellum years of the nineteenth century, while no inconsiderable achievement, was hardly sufficient to make more than a small dent in the low-income problems of its overwhelmingly rural-agricultural population. Little wonder that the planter class—once freed by the defeat of the Populists and the disenfranchisement movements of the nineties from the threat of the insurgent lower-class whites—was no longer so easily whipped into line by its erstwhile industrialist allies. Their political dominance once more assured, the planters could now revert to their old agrarian values. If they now attacked "the interests," they did so not only because they were appealing to the remnants of Populist radicalism held by their lesser farm neighbors but also because most of them no longer saw any personal advantage in further Southern industrial development.

The modest success which the New South movement had enjoyed by 1900 in achieving regional industrialization does not gainsay that basically it was on the right track. Despite its slogans, extravagances, and excesses, the drive to industrialize was truly the only hope for the South's rural poverty. While many of the advocates of the New South had axes to grind, there were other prominent Southerners without any personal interest in the outcome whose analyses of the seventies were just as valid in 1900 and later. In 1872, for example, a high state education official of Tennessee, J. B. Killebrew, had deplored the fact that "one person in the

24 to 29 percent; and Tennessee's (with relatively little textile development) from 28 to 29 percent. During the same period, Ohio's increase was from 82 to 124 percent and Iowa's (already favored by its very rich agricultural base) from 29 to 38 percent. In 1900 the non-Southern states were 50 percent urban and in 1920 had only 18 percent of their gainfully employed population in agriculture.

The migration data are compiled from Lee *et al., Population Redistribution and Economic Growth,* Table P-1. The states included are Kentucky, Tennessee, Alabama, Mississippi, Louisiana, Virginia, North Carolina, South Carolina, and Georgia. During the same period, Arkansas, Texas, and Oklahoma had a net gain by inmigration of nearly 1,200,000 people, 85 percent white.

rigorous climate and poor soil of Massachusetts [produces] nearly three times as much as one in the rich fields and genial climate of [Tennessee]," and he advocated the creation of an educated working class as the basis for higher labor productivity and industrial prosperity in the South. In 1875, Tennessee's commissioner of agriculture, William H. Jackson, joined him in emphasizing that manufacturing was the proper remedy for the economic debility of the state's agriculture. In rebuttal to the region's traditional agrarianism, Jackson noted that in England, the most affluent nation on earth, farm people numbered but a third of the total population.[7] Such wise and perceptive people as these Tennesseeans were far ahead of their time.

Unfortunately, much of the early industrialization in the South was of an exploitative kind, frequently depending heavily upon child labor and even convict labor. Reconstruction was generally followed by coalition state governments of industrialists and planters. These men took retrenchment as their watchword and, "often describing themselves as the 'rule of the taxpayer,' frankly constituted themselves champions of the property owner against the propertyless and allegedly untaxed masses.... Cheapness, even niggardliness, ... became widely accepted as the criterion of good government.... *Laissez faire* became almost a test of Southern patriotism."[8] The public-school funds were the principal victim of retrenchment and laissez faire, policies which were reinforced by the strong commitment of the new textile magnates to a system of child labor and by the continued opposition of the planter class to the idea of schools for the masses.

While such men as Killebrew found that their advocacy of industrialization was wholly acceptable to the dominant New South forces, the latter turned a deaf ear to their concomitant pleas for the support of mass education, which if heeded might easily have accelerated the rate of Southern industrial development far beyond its actual confines. This does not mean that the principal fault of the early New South movement was its exploitative and laissez faire character. The initial industrial development of England and

New England had not been dissimilar. The difference lay in the fact that Southern industrial development only gradually evolved, without ever attaining the proportions of a revolution. Having once fallen behind industrially, the South lacked the entrepreneurial talent, skilled artisans, and other external economies whose presence in the already industrially established North tended to make industrialization there self-generating. In the absence of such factors, it was the old agrarian pattern—only slightly modified by the development of such low-skill manufactures as textiles—which tended to be self-generating in the South. With scores of poor and ignorant farm workers continuing to stand in line for every new factory job, the social forces which would have favored an ever-increasing investment in the quality of the people and an ever-widening spread of the benefits of progress were kept under control in the South. In the factory as on the plantation, the general Southern outlook continued to be conservative, paternalistic, and backward-looking.

To sum up this brief and inadequate historical analysis, we may say with a considerable degree of oversimplification that when the ante-bellum agrarian South could have industrialized, it did not want to; when the post-bellum prostrate South decided belatedly that it did want industrialization, its sudden frenzied efforts to achieve it met with only limited success; and when its limited success had become apparent, it tended to return to the old agrarian values which had prevailed before the Civil War.

The New Southern Agrarianism: Progress Condemned

DURING 1900-1930, the South's urban population increased from 18 to 34 percent of its people. In 1930, its relative share of the nation's total value added by manufacture was about the same as

27

it had been in 1900 and 1860. These figures mean that in absolute terms the South's industrial development had kept pace with a rapidly developing nation. On the other hand, in 1930 the South's per capita value added by manufacture was still only 37 percent of the national average * and only 30 percent of the average for the non-South. More important, its per capita income was still only 43 percent of the non-South's. Primarily as a result of continued relatively low incomes, ten Southern states during 1900-1930 lost nearly 3,500,000 people (52 percent white) by net outmigration to other regions.† With two-thirds of its population rural and 43 percent of its workers engaged in agriculture, the South of 1930 was still predominantly rural-agricultural, its development having continued to lag far behind that of the rest of the nation.

Only within such a historical context can one understand how, as late as 1930, a group of intelligent Southerners could have noted "the melancholy fact that the South itself has wavered a little and shown signs of wanting to join up behind the common or American industrial ideal." In opposing this tendency, the Vanderbilt Agrarians sought to persuade "the younger Southerners, who are being converted frequently to the industrial gospel, [to] come back to the support of the Southern tradition" and "to look very critically at the advantages of becoming a 'new South' which will be only an undistinguished replica of the usual industrial community." ⁹

The Agrarians' indictment of industrialism charged that through it science was applied to make labor intense, mercenary, servile, and insecure, instead of something to be performed with leisure and enjoyment; to create overproduction, unemployment, and greater inequality in the distribution of wealth which could lead only to

* The corresponding figures for selected states were as follows: South Carolina 37 percent, Georgia 41 percent, Tennessee 48 percent, Virginia (42 percent in 1900) 60 percent, Ohio 175 percent, and Iowa 50 percent.

† Same source and same states (plus Arkansas) as cited previously. During the same period Oklahoma, Texas, and Florida gained by net inmigration 1,500,000 people (89 percent white).

the superstate; to destroy that relation of man to nature which is conducive to a flourishing religion and vital creative arts; to develop relations between man and man unfavorable to such amenities of life as good manners, hospitality, family life, and romantic love; and to accelerate the tempo and instability of life by a never-ending race between material goods, human wants, and human effort.[10]

If it is easy to see what the Agrarians were against, it is far more difficult to see what they were for. They particularly deplored those products of industrialization which, "applied at the expense of agriculture,... have reduced the part of the population supporting itself upon the soil to a smaller and smaller fraction." In opposition, they espoused the theory of agrarianism under which "the culture of the soil is the best and most sensitive of vocations, and ... therefore ... should have the economic preference and enlist the maximum number of workers." Thus, concerned with ethics but ignoring economics, they re-echoed Jefferson's proposed index of corruption—which had held that the ratio of a state's nonfarmers to its farmers measured "the proportion of its unsound to its healthy parts" [11]—and tried to resurrect the romantic diatribes of Carlyle and Ruskin against "the Dismal Science."

Lacking an economist among their numbers, the Vanderbilt group depended upon a psychologist, Lyle H. Lanier, for its supporting economic analysis. Undoubtedly strongly influenced by the large army of urban unemployed at that time—a floating population "unattached to that tremendous social anchor, land"—Lanier saw no solution for overproduction and technological unemployment except a renunciation of "the capitalistic industrial program." Even so, "further mechanization of industrial production should be encouraged, since this would mean that progressively fewer persons would be required for its processes ... and the large surplus of chronically unemployed should be induced by all means to return to agriculture." To the objection that "already there is over-production of agricultural commodities," Lanier replied that agriculture is more than a process of production, since it offers to "millions of people who now hang on to the fringes of industry ...

a place to live and food to eat ... [and] a base on which to knit together the fragments of [their broken] lives." *

If the Agrarians appeared to be primarily occupied with essentially aristocratic values and virtues, such views as Lanier's make clear that the agrarian ideal meant to some of them millions of small landholding, independent, and self-sufficient yeoman farmers —an American peasantry—rather than the rich planters of Southern romantic tradition. Thus, Andrew Nelson Lytle deplored the economic institutions and events which had led Southern farmers "deeper into the money economy instead of freeing them"; he admitted that they had nonetheless established a satisfactory but uneasy compromise between commercial and subsistence production, but warned that "The next, the fatal step, is to become a progressive farmer, for then he must ... think first of a money economy, last of ... farming as a way of life." What was needed, according to Ransom, was a return to the anti-materialistic tradition under which the Southerner enveloped "both his work and his play with a leisure which permitted the activity of intelligence ... [in a] comfortable and rural sort of establishment." [12]

While most of the Agrarians of *I'll Take My Stand* idealized the Old South and its aristocratic tradition, with an occasional bow toward the small landholding yeoman farmer, they seemed abysmally unaware (Robert Penn Warren being the major exception) of the vast numbers of Negro and white sharecroppers who were the real forgotten men of Southern agriculture. Perhaps stung by

---

* Twelve Southerners, *I'll Take My Stand*, pp. 150, 151-52. I hope that Lanier, who is a good friend of mine, will forgive my resurrecting this better-forgotten excursion into economic analysis, whose shaky foundations he would probably now readily admit, distinguished psychologist and social scientist that he is. It is interesting to note, however, the similarity between his position and that of John Stuart Mill (*Principles of Political Economy*, Book I, Chapter XII, Section 3), both of whom saw in the increasing efficiency of industrial production the hope of transferring nonfarm workers back into agriculture, although the problem to be solved thereby had meanwhile shifted from Malthusian poverty to industrial and agricultural plenty.

criticisms to this effect, those of the Vanderbilt group who joined with some less esoteric and more practical men in the writing of *Who Owns America?* had by 1936 given considerable ground. Having in this second book reduced their nebulous doctrines to a political program, they directed their principal darts at "monopoly capitalism" and its manifestations in big business and big planters alike.

As might have been expected, Donald Davidson conceded least. Attributing the South's war of independence to the Northern imperialism which sought to bring about "the substitution of a factory system for a plantation system in Virginia," Davidson deplored the South's status since its defeat as a subject province under the reign of "the regional imperialism of the Northeast." To be sure, the South had eroded lands, "devilish" one-crop and tenant systems, and an illiterate, diseased, and apathetic population. But the reason was the "distant tyranny of money" under which the South and the West went "in overalls that the Northeast may walk in silk and satin." When it came to political solutions, however, Davidson was extremely vague. He toyed with the idea of new regional commonwealths with the power to impose interregional tariffs, to tax or regulate "foreign" capital and "foreign" monopolies, to control credit and money, to protect regional educational systems against outside rule, to prevent absentee ownership of farm lands, and "to preserve [a] bi-racial social system without the furtive evasion or raw violence to which it is now driven when sniped at with weapons of Federal legality." He also suggested that such regional commonwealths "be given a veto power in certain instances, some modern equivalent of Calhoun's principle of nullification." In any case, he concluded, "Whatever restores small property, fosters agrarianism, and curtails exaggerated industrialism is on the side of regional autonomy" and speeds "the end of colonialism." [13]

The burden of the attack on the big-business planters was carried by a new recruit to the Agrarian ranks, George Marion O'Donnell. According to O'Donnell, the big-business planters had willfully connived with the villainous plantation system, "deserting the agrarian economy deliberately in order to share in the great profits of a money economy dominated by finance-capitalism." However, "more important than financial abuses, perhaps, are the unfortunate living conditions among tenants on great Southern cotton plantations," particularly in Texas and the Mississippi Delta: "These people are on the soil, to be sure, but they are essentially industrial workers—and badly treated industrial workers at that. The instruments of production are all controlled by the capitalist (the landlord); the labor is hard, and regular, though not so unvarying as the work in a factory; farmers are not attached to the soil by emotional ties; the whole system is 'efficient' and impersonal." [14]

Certainly, O'Donnell continued, alongside the mass-producing plantations are agrarian planters who share with their tenants (not sharecroppers) an agrarian economy where "labor is varied, crops are diversified, and the aim of the work is not to make enormous profits." But these agrarian planters, who must sell some cotton for cash to pay for taxes and basic supplies, face a market glutted by the big-business planters, which constantly pressures them to desert agrarianism for specialized cotton production. O'Donnell was hopeful that the whole system of mass production in cotton might eventually disappear. In any case, he made clear his belief that the most important and neglected class of farmer was the yeoman farmer, "a lesser freeholder who cultivates his own land." It was the yeoman—largely of the frontier tradition and the hills rather than the slaveholding tradition and the delta, part capitalist and part laborer—for whose benefit plans should be made. Public policy should be directed toward assisting small farmers and helping tenants to become yeomen, thereby restoring "liberty based on property." [15]

Lytle and Ransom particularly enlarged upon this theme of the heroic yeoman farmer, much along the lines of their essays in the earlier book. Others attacked with equal vigor the domination of big business over small business in manufacturing and the distributive trades, the concentration of corporate wealth, and the separation of business ownership and control, and here as in agriculture they advocated public policies which would put "private property back into the hands of the disinherited American people." Some of the Fugitive poets now having become Agrarian politicians, *Who Owns America?* represented a kind of right-wing radicalism quite within the heritage of the old Southern Populist Movement. The Agrarians now showed a commendable passion for social justice (at least for *white* men) that was woefully absent in their earlier book. However, whatever their intent, the net effect of their attack continued to be a condemnation of economic progress in most of its aspects. They were writing, of course, at a time when the beliefs of all America in future progress had been shaken to their foundations and when even prominent economists considered "economic stagnation" a more realistic assumption. Nonetheless, with the benefit of our hindsight, it is clear that both the Agrarians and the stagnation economists laid down guidelines for future policy which if followed would have been quite inconsistent with national or regional economic progress.

The Agrarian program would have segmented a national economy whose major asset had been its vast free-trade area; it would have revived and strengthened the South's negative and destructive spirit of sectionalism; and it would have reduced to an even slower pace the industrial-urban development and agricultural progress which are essential if we are to solve the South's serious problem of poverty. Thus, the Agrarian program would have perpetuated the historical inability of most Southerners, farmers or otherwise, to participate fully in the rising American level of material well-being. While man does not live by bread alone, a modicum of material well-being is for most men a necessary condition for their finding the good life. The Agrarians were utterly sincere in wanting for most Southerners the good life, perhaps even including some greater measure of the world's riches. Unfortunately, as economists they were abominable advisers on the means of achieving greater material well-being. As humanists, however, they had (and still have) much to offer in showing all of us how to use the

33

fruits of economic progress, once achieved, as means to the more spiritual side of a good, full, and happy life.

Agrarian Values as a Barrier to Progress

I FEEL THAT only a Southerner born and bred can fully appreciate the intensity of feeling with which most Southerners hunger for possessing the soil, love outdoor life, and appreciate leisure. That such agrarian values have persisted so long in the South in itself offers ample testimony to the slow if steady pace of the region's industrial-urban development. Yet the persistence of agrarian values has been not only the result but in some degree at least the cause of a laggard Southern economy.

In the South as in most underdeveloped countries, the dominant agrarian values long supported a scale of social prestige which placed the landowner, the religious leader, the military leader, and the political leader at the top and the man of business far down the line. If, as I believe to be true, the South has invested a disproportionate share of its indigenous capital in less productive agricultural assets relative to more productive business assets and has directed more of its superior human talent into nonbusiness fields than have other regions, its traditionally low view of the businessman and industrialist (the extravagances of the early New South movement notwithstanding) is probably in substantial part accountable. As a result, much of the South's business leadership has been furnished, if at all, from such minorities as migratory Yankees and Southern highlanders, who have been reared in other traditions.* The result-

* There appears to have been a striking increase in the importance of Northerners in Nashville's business leadership in the last decade. Howard Beers's research in the origins of the business leaders of Lexington, Ky., has revealed that a surprisingly large number had their roots in the mountains of

ing dearth of indigenous business leadership has also protected the large landowner (and even certain industrialists) from new forces which would inevitably weaken his political and economic hold on his rural community, reduce the cheap labor supply so essential to his comfortable way of life, and increase the general public concern for improving the lot of his less privileged neighbors. While the Southern business leader's social status has undoubtedly gradually improved, his ascent has not been an easy one in view of Southern tradition.

Love of the land and outdoor life has seriously impeded the resource adjustments which are an essential part of the process of Southern economic development. It has discouraged low-income rural people from migrating to better economic opportunities elsewhere. It has caused those who have migrated to hang onto their small home acreages, allowing their land to return to brush and bush, instead of selling it to their land-hungry neighbors. It has perpetuated an increasingly ill-founded belief that the South's rural poor need cause no concern since "they like to hunt and fish anyway." Such a belief has salved the consciences of wealthier planter neighbors and landlords in their moments of feeling an unaccustomed social responsibility and, by building the reputation

---

eastern Kentucky. (Cf. my article, "Accommodating Economic Change in Underdeveloped Countries," p. 158.) Over the years, the generally high caliber of Southern members of the United States Senate (excepting of course the occasional demagogue) relative to those from the Midwest probably has similarly reflected not only a narrower electorate but the higher prestige which Southern voters have traditionally accorded politics.

To be sure, in a laggard economy such as the South's, it is quite possible that high social prestige and relatively high income are positively correlated. In a capital-short region, occupations heavily dependent upon capital (business enterprise) tend to yield low returns to the persons so engaged unless they are themselves men of means. On the other hand, certain professions (military, political, religious) yield to the persons so engaged returns which are little affected by capital scarcity; other occupations (the landlord) may even benefit from the high labor-capital ratio. Hence, the social prestige of particular occupations may in part rest upon an economic base.

that such low-income people are unsuited to the discipline of a factory system, has discouraged decisions to industrialize rural communities.

Leisure as a dominant agrarian value has too often become a cover-up for lack of enterprise and even sheer laziness among Southerners. There is much in the Southern tradition of "gracious living" which has permeated the whole Southern society and has made life more pleasant and enjoyable for all. But this does not controvert the fact that Southern leisureliness, hospitality, and good manners had their origins in an agrarian aristocracy to whom a wealth of land and slaves permitted the luxuries of leisure and hospitality. If there was leisure among wealthy planters, it was a leisure won by the sweat of black men's brows. If there was hospitality, it was frequently selective according to family blood-lines (as was the Yankee's hospitality selective according to wealth) rather than that more genuine if less lavish hospitality of the Westerner who accepted every man on his own merits.

If there were good manners, they existed in part because in a society in which every man had his place, manners were a necessary component in playing the role to which one had been assigned by birth—whether master or servant, lord or serf. Furthermore, manners were a practical necessity if the planter was to handle his workers in his own economic interest. The Yankee industrialist did not have to be courteous to a machine and he found cash wages a partial substitute for verbal persuasion as an incentive to his labor force. In the Southern agrarian society "the manners of the ladies and gentlemen were in part the fine flower of that rough courtesy which got the cotton picked and the cane ground." [16] The Negro or poor white's courtesy was too often that of a menial or subservient person who clearly knew "which side his bread was buttered on."

Thanks to its agrarian-aristocratic origins, "suspicion of the Calvinistic-Puritanical-Yankee notion of 'work-for-work's sake' " became one of the dominant Southern traits. Calhoun's "wise and masterly inactivity" was more to the Southern taste.[17] Such was certainly the model to which the Vanderbilt Agrarians pointed in defining an agrarian society as "one in which agriculture is the leading vocation, whether for wealth, for pleasure, or for prestige—a form of labor that is pursued with intelligence and leisure." [18] If the Agrarians were thinking of Jefferson or Calhoun as their prototype of the contemplative Southern gentleman, such genius was of a type woefully rare even in ante-bellum days. While higher education in the Old South was pre-eminently education for the planter aristocracy, with the objective of combining "intelligence with leisure," it certainly did not long succeed in achieving this goal.

Significantly, it was because Jefferson felt that his alma mater, William and Mary, had given too much priority to leisure over intelligence that he took the initiative in founding the University of Virginia,[19] and it is probable that by 1875 (if not 1860) he would have found the latter institution faulty on similar grounds. Nor should Jefferson's early interest in universal common-school education, so long neglected in the South, be forgotten. Lacking this kind of education and unable to afford private-school education, neither the yeoman farmers nor the poor whites could generally bring much except native intelligence to bear upon their leisure time, and there is even considerable doubt that (with their more Calvinistic persuasions and harder lot) the yeomen even had much leisure time to spare.

In fact, for the great masses of Southerners, leisure was probably from early days a virtue by necessity rather than by choice. If they were small landowners they lacked sufficient resources to keep them busy more than half of the year. If they were slaves or sharecroppers the near impossibility of advancing themselves by their own efforts bred inefficiency, lassitude, and improvidence. In either case, except insofar as hunting and fishing were a necessity in order to have meat on the table, leisure time was much more likely to be passed in rowdiness and brawling than in intellectual pursuits. (Not all delinquents are either juvenile or urban.) As against the Agrarians' intelligent man of leisure, the truer view would appear to be Walter Hines Page's observation that "the one thing that differentiates the mass of Southern men from the mass of Massachusetts men, say, is this lack of intellectual curiosity." Or, in the damning words of the editor of the *Progressive Farmer*, Clarence H. Poe, "Your untrained, inefficient man is not only a poverty-breeder for himself, but the contagion of it curses every man in the community that is guilty of leaving him untrained." [20] In view of its origins, the tradition of leisure has been a doubtful virtue, discouraging economic enterprise on the part of the large landowners and producing, and even giving sanction to, laziness on the part of poor whites and Negroes.

Even so, the effects of the Southern love of outdoor life and leisure on the suitability of low-income farm people for industrial employment have been seriously exaggerated, not only by Northerners, whose ignorance might be understood if not forgiven, but by upper-class Southerners who claim the authority of "knowing their own people." It is true that Southerners, particularly upland freeholding small farmers, feel particularly strong ties to their family and their home community which make them especially reluctant to leave agriculture if it means a change of residence. But most of them are eager to shift to part-time farming if nearby industrial employment becomes available. The plain fact is that local nonfarm employment opportunities in most Southern rural communities are "rationed" in the sense that far more farm people would be happy to take local nonfarm jobs at prevailing wages if these jobs were available. Time and again, officials of Southern industrial development commissions have reported applications for local industrial employment 10 to 20 times greater than the openings which resulted from establishing even a relatively large new plant in a rural area. Nor have the employees of such a plant shown a lack of capacity and adaptability in their new jobs. Despite a high rate of outmigration which might have been expected to be selective in leaving behind those with a high preference for leisure and with less initiative and ability, industrialists with actual operating experience in the South have found its labor force highly satis-factory.[21]

The South's Agrarian romanticists might therefore recall Prince Henry's wise words (*Henry IV*, Part I) about the unyoked humor of idleness:

> If all the year were playing holidays,
> To sport would be as tedious as to work....

Leisure, like more tangible things, is subject to the law of diminishing utility. Because of the abundant supply of underemployed rural labor in the South, those who hunt and fish by preference, rather than by reason of the lack of more lucrative uses of their time, are still a distinct minority. Only if rural people are given practical alternatives can their alleged preference for leisure be put to the test. Insofar as such a preference is genuine, it can be expected to change as their general pattern of wants changes in response to the increased availability of a wider range of goods and services and to their realization that with greater effort they can themselves finally hope to attain a higher level of living. There are those who sneer at the ubiquitous television aerials in our rural slums. Properly considered, however, this phenomenon may clearly make (through its positive effect on incentives) its own substantial contribution to regional economic progress.

The South's persistent agrarianism has been a major factor in perpetuating a federal agricultural policy which has given little help to the small farmer while seriously interfering with the resource adjustments needed to achieve a more efficient and progressive agriculture. It is no accident that of the six commodities which have received especially favorable treatment under our farm price-support program, four (cotton, tobacco, peanuts, and rice) are Southern farm products. It is also no accident that most Southern Congressmen have been among those most stubbornly resisting corrective amendments to this depression-born and increasingly malfunctioning farm program. That they have resisted has undoubtedly reflected not only the strong agrarian values of their

39

constituents but, more often than not, their own personal convictions that they are helping Southern farmers, small as well as large. (I believe, for example, that Congressman Pace of Georgia was not merely grandstanding when he publicly condemned my criticisms of the economics of the parity-price concept in 1945 by declaring that "Parity is as sacred as the Sermon on the Mount!")

Whatever the beliefs and motivations of these congressmen, the facts clearly belie their professions. Nothing is more futile than the attempt to raise significantly the income of the small farmer by price supports, since he has so little to sell. For example, year after year, the cotton price-support program has put scores of thousands of dollars into the pockets of a few large planters (who are far better off than the typical urban family) in order to add a hundred or two to the average farmer's gross income. In the Delta area of the Old Cotton Belt, 50 percent of the benefits of the lavishly wasteful cotton program have accrued to the owners and share-croppers of only 5 percent of the landholding units.*

As a partial offset, Congress has sought to protect the small farmer from increasingly drastic acreage controls by establishing a minimum acreage allotment, with the consequence that the larger farmers and planters have borne the brunt of further acreage cut-backs. Even so, the benefits to the small farmer have been extremely meager. For example, the small Burley tobacco farmer is typically allowed to produce 0.7 acres of leaf, which means, even at high support prices, only about $700 of gross income. This is usually his only significant source of cash farm income, from which he must purchase his seed, fertilizer, and other necessary production items. Thus, even acreage allotments which have discriminated

---

* William H. Nicholls, "Multiple-Unit Operations and Gross Farm Income Distribution within the Old Cotton Belt," *Southern Economic Journal*, XIX (1953), 477-79. The following examples of the average amount of the five largest CCC loans (in effect, total government purchase payments) and the average CCC loan to farmers on the 1953 cotton crop are typical: Mississippi $479,535 and $372; Tennessee $42,655 and $299, and Georgia $27,516 and $309!

against the more efficient larger farmers and cotton-producing areas have been incapable of producing a satisfactory income for the small farmer. In combination with high price supports which encourage chronic overproduction, acreage allotments have been a serious impediment to the achievement of an efficient Southern agriculture. Worst of all, because of its extremely high cost, the farm price-support program has diverted public funds and public concern from a million or more low-income farm families who require substantial and sustained public assistance, not to help them stay in agriculture but to help them to find more remunerative employment in nonagricultural occupations.

It is a law of economic history (for regions as well as nations) that economic progress, broadly viewed, is associated with a decline in the relative importance of agriculture. For those who value progress, the South's disproportionately heavy dependence on agriculture has been a sound indicator of its backwardness, not a matter for congratulation. As a leading agricultural economist, Joseph S. Davis, put it:

> It is no longer inevitable that declining relative importance of agriculture should involve the loss of all virtues associated with farming. . . . In a broad view of a nation's welfare, it appears unwise to maintain an unnecessarily large farming population, with attendant problems of excessive output of farm products or low standards of living of subsistence farmers, in order that rural living may be enjoyed by a larger fraction of the population. From the standpoint of maximum satisfaction of wants it is desirable, not undesirable, to have as small a proportion of the total energy as possible devoted to provision for essential wants, so as to leave the maximum available for leisure activities and satisfaction of wants for wholesome nonessentials.[22]

Such a view does not mean the total rejection of the Agrarian ideal of a yeoman farmer. Most economists of agriculture still accept this ideal in the sense of a middle-class farmer who owns and operates his own land with adequate capital and with little dependence upon labor beyond that of his own family. Unlike the Agrarian, however, the economist wants for that farmer sufficient acreage and other capital resources to permit him to use modern machinery efficiently, to employ the most progressive techniques, and to find the most satisfactory combination of crops and livestock for his particular situation. Such a farmer will operate on a largely commercial rather than subsistence basis but will be productive enough to earn as much as in comparable nonfarm occupations. With such an ideal, the economist further recognizes the necessity of reducing the farm population substantially by helping those who prefer to leave agriculture to find better economic opportunities elsewhere; and the equally important necessity of helping those who choose to remain in agriculture to find sufficient capital to make their farms productive and remunerative. The economic facts of life are such that the South must choose which it wants—many poor and inefficient farmers or perhaps a fourth as many who are prosperous and progressive. The romantic views of the Agrarians notwithstanding, we cannot possibly have it both ways.

CHAPTER

3

THE RIGIDITY OF THE SOCIAL STRUCTURE

Malvolio. I know my place as I would they should do theirs. . . .

—Shakespeare, *Twelfth Night*

WHILE the structure of most of American society has been firmly based on the democratic principle, the South instead chose the aristocratic principle inherited from its predominantly British forebears. A priori, the case for the aristocratic principle is, of course, just as plausible as the case for the democratic principle: both seek the welfare of the community and disagree only as to the means of bringing it about. In practice, however, the leaders of most aristocratic societies (such as the French nobility of the *ancien regime*) have plundered the people, have known many privileges but few duties, and have had a purely selfish and pleasure-loving outlook on life. Fortunately for the South, the English model was an exception. The means by which the English aristocracy acquired its landed wealth were not without their shady side, leading as they did to the virtual destruction of the rural yeomanry. Nevertheless, because this aristocracy came to accept fully the concept of *noblesse oblige*, it produced the finest flower

43

of aristocratic culture which the Western world has known. To the English aristocrat, wealth and property did not remain ends in themselves but became means to the obligatory end of serving all the people. As a result, the view that *noblesse oblige*—and, conversely, that carrying out one's obligations ennobles—became the accepted ideal of the great masses of the English people.[1]

The great length of time in which the English aristocracy remained viable undoubtedly reflects both the firmness with which it held to *noblesse oblige* and the flexibility with which it constantly absorbed new blood. The original aristocracy—whose wealth and prestige was based on land ownership—survived by assimilating the rising commercial and industrial class of *nouveaux riches*, many of whom in turn adopted the ideals, customs, and way of life of the older aristocrats. Nor did the English aristocratic system prevent the development during the nineteenth century of a proud, vigorous, and class-conscious middle class upon which so much of English economic development came to depend. Thus, England was governed by a tolerant aristocracy which was open to new ideas, hence inclusive rather than exclusive, with a gradually broadening base and the ability to choose the right moment for every compromise which its continued supremacy necessitated.[2]

To what extent did the Southern aristocratic system succeed in emulating this English model? Insofar as it failed, what were the reasons and the consequences? It is with these important questions that we shall be concerned in this chapter.

The Rise of a Landed Aristocracy

IN THE England of the seventeenth and eighteenth centuries, land ownership was the key to social prestige and to economic and political privilege. The sheer abundance of land in the American

44

colonies naturally suggested the establishment of hereditary landed estates and resulted in the granting of large tracts of land to friends of the Crown. With the American Revolution the manorial system of land disposition largely gave way to a more democratic land-settlement pattern. In sharp contrast with most Latin-American countries, the United States avoided the concentration of land ownership and the rise of a socio-politically dominant landed class. Instead, by combining an equalitarian land policy with vast outlays for internal improvements and encouragement of the formation of new interior states, the new nation settled an entire continent with remarkable dispatch.[3]

Once again the course of Southern history took a turn at variance with national trends. By the time of the American Revolution, the pattern of a landed aristocracy was already firmly established in the Tidewater areas of the Southern colonies. The struggle of small farmers of the Piedmont against the domination of the Tidewater aristocrats had therefore only begun in 1776. In fact, even the apparent victory of frontier equalitarianism over the commercial and planter classes of the seaboard in the Jacksonian era was largely aborted in the Southeastern states. Long before then, Kentucky and Tennessee had won the status of new states only by accepting constitutions which were modelled after the conservative constitutions of Virginia and North Carolina and by recognizing prior land claims which robbed them of an adequate basis for financing common schools and internal improvements. Further south, planters had already pushed westward seeking new cotton lands, displacing many of the pioneer small farmers who had preceded them.

Wherever land and climate were suitable for the rich new combination of cotton, slavery, and plantation, a new planter aristocracy tended to emerge. Even in these plantation areas, small farmers continued to constitute the bulk of the population, but they increasingly came under the social and political domination of the new planter class. The latter strongly resisted measures to broaden the suffrage, to establish *ad valorem* taxation of land (and slaves) for the general welfare, and to provide free universal public-school education at a time when these democratizing influences were greatly strengthening the socio-economic foundations of the more progressive Middle West. In the process, they effectively insulated themselves from social and political forces which might otherwise have been their undoing and continued to set the goals to which lesser men at least aspired.

There were in every Southern state, particularly in the Upper South, hilly areas whose physical characteristics and economic isolation brought a diversified type of general farming not conducive to large slaveholdings. In such areas, there was a more democratic social structure in which the larger farmers enjoyed a position distinctly superior to that of their cotton-planter counterparts of the middle class and in which even the poor and self-sufficient highlanders escaped the social ostracism and menial position of the poor whites in the plantation regions. Long before the Civil War, the highlanders had found common cause against the planter-dominated governments in their state capitals, but their sectional interests continued to be largely neglected until 1860.[4] Despite such intersectional conflicts of interest within the South, the ante-bellum Southern planter class (like its English counterpart) maintained its power primarily by persuasion and example rather than by fraud or force. How was such an easy conquest of the frontier spirit of equalitarianism possible?

The English aristocratic system came more naturally to Southerners than to other new Americans. As John Crowe Ransom put it, "the [strain] which determined the peculiar tradition of the South was the one which came out of Europe most convinced of the virtues of establishment, contrasting with those strains which seem for the most part to have dominated the other sections, and which came out of Europe feeling rebellious toward all establishments." [5] With such beginnings, the South's subsequent history of plantation and slavery created an environment unusually favorable to the creation of a thoroughly stratified society in which first the Negro, and later the typical white, had his place. The end result, said Ashmore, was: "a set of conventions accepted by both races and providing the basis for an orderly if uneven social structure. Fundamentally, the relationship was that of master and servant. At its worst it worked great hardships and gross cruelties upon those cast in the lesser role. At its best it embodied the concept of *noblesse oblige* and carried with it the obligation of the strong to sustain the weak." [6]

The "Southern gentleman" early became an ideal type to which many Southerners aspired and which nearly all respected. In Ronald F. Howell's sympathetic portrayal, this ideal gentleman of Southern tradition was characterized as one who is

> tolerant, kindly, broad-minded, non-puritan, moderate, hospitable, and courteous. His ethics are . . . religiously oriented (frequently . . . cast in an Anglican mold), and his politics . . . non-doctrinaire. . . . he is a man of parts, catholic interests, and large compassion. A totally integrated personality, he is also supremely gregarious . . . [with] a sense of purpose and continuity. More concerned with *being* and *thinking* than *doing*, he has a critical though genial view of life. His character is well-balanced and honorable . . . [and] boasts the spiritual lineage of the English Cavalier. . . . Nevertheless his status society, while properly aristocratic and conservative, does not reject the democratic principle of equality of opportunity. Translating "aristocracy" literally as the "rule of the best" and understanding by "conservatism" the philosophy of "preserving" the best, it restricts the highest offices not to the "rich and well born" but to the most qualified and deserving, wherever they are found. . . . [Finally, it accepts] the classical Greek concept of the gentleman as the man of virtue whose natural function is social and political participation. [7]

This ideal type of the Virginia and South Carolina colonial gentry was clearly as English as bully beef and plum pudding. If the Tidewater gentry had had to depend only upon its own progeny, it would soon have lost its social and political influence in a young South which, thanks to plentiful lands on the frontier, was still vertically mobile. However, so powerful was the aristocratic ideal, Tidewater model, that it become the goal which many Southern backwoodsmen-turned-planters sought to emulate. Even if such men were not aristocrats by birth (Jefferson Davis is a prime example), their success in acquiring sufficient land and slaves to the south and west made it possible for them to imitate the older Tidewater gentry and set themselves up for aristocrats on their own account. That they were able to get away with such pretensions was abetted by the growing conflict with the Yankee, which encouraged the entire South, in Cash's colorful words, "to wrap itself in contemptuous superiority, to sneer down the Yankee as low-bred, crass, and money-grubbing, and even to beget in his bourgeois soul a kind of secret and envious awe." Even if the ideal of the Southern gentleman was overdrawn and extravagant, it was what most new cotton planters seriously saw themselves as being and what a handful of the best endowed of them actually came somewhere near becoming.[8]

The new planter class did accept a considerable measure of *noblesse oblige* toward the commoner whites about them. Their expressions of this strong sense of obligation were frequently paternalistic and condescending, however, and in part motivated by frequent blood bonds of kinship with their less successful neighbors and by the primitive necessity of sharing with all other white men a feeling of common superiority over the Negro slave. In the process, the aristocratic ideal and its concepts of honor and standards of conduct came to be adopted in a simpler and more attractive form by the yeoman class and were not without their influence (at least in primitive ways) even upon the poor whites. Most yeomen and poor whites tended in return to confirm by acquiescence their belief in the planters' own noble professions of integrity and social responsibility. The result of these attitudes was a general acceptance by lesser whites of a planter-dominated status society, the concomitant lack of class feeling infuriating would-be Yankee agitators as much as the comparable English situation did most American observers.

The Corruption of the Aristocratic Ideal

IF AT its best such *noblesse oblige* represents the highest product of an aristocratic social framework, Cash showed that as it developed in the South it had a distinctly negative side as well. It became alloyed with a frontier individualism which, "while willing enough to ameliorate the specific instance, relentlessly laid down as its basic social postulate the doctrine that every man was completely and wholly responsible for himself." The result was that most members of the planter class developed a thoroughgoing self-satisfaction such that even when they took most seriously their sense of responsibility for the masses, they assumed that their own interest was identical with that of the common white and "gave him advice, told him what to think, from that standpoint." Rarely did one of them ever even slightly apprehend "that the general shiftlessness and degradation of the masses was a social product" or concern himself about measures which might systematically raise his economic and social level.[9]

Such attitudes differed little from those of the pre-industrial English aristocracy and probably would have had less pernicious long-run effects if the peculiar American institution of slavery had not become the underpinning of a social structure already showing increasingly hierarchical tendencies. Unfortunately, as the planter class felt an ever-mounting need to justify slavery, it tended to turn to a philosophy of caste in which slavery was divinely ordained and every white man also had his place. Like slavery itself, the philosophy which grew up in its defense was brutalizing in its effects on the minds and spirits of planters and poor whites alike. This doctrine served "to strengthen and expand the planter's narrow class pride, to increase his private contempt for the common whites, to ratify his complacency and harden toward arrogance" his growing conviction "that it was his *right* to instruct and com-

49

mand." At the same time, it diverted from the planters to the Negro slave the wrath of the poor whites at the "white-trash" epithet.[10]

This does not mean, of course, that class lines were ever completely rigid in the ante-bellum South. Particularly as long as there remained good new cotton lands to settle, low-born men were able to move up into the planter class and even to become accepted as aristocrats. In an almost completely agrarian society, however, the period of social mobility in any given area was at most a few decades, after which westward migration offered the only significant avenue of escape for the less successful. For those who remained behind, upward mobility soon became extremely difficult in the face of the local scarcity of land and the development of local mores which actively supported social immobility.

Even so, the Southern white social structure which resulted was by no means composed only of planters and poor whites. Within the South's agrarian society, there was always a substantial middle class of yeoman farmers. It was just such sturdy, self-reliant, and self-respecting middle-class farmers who contributed so much to the democratization and general economic development of the North and West. Even in the South, they were vastly greater in numbers than were the large planters. Unfortunately, before the Civil War, the yeomen of the plantation belt were largely brought under the political sway of their larger planter neighbors while the much more numerous and locally dominant yeomen of the non-plantation hill country found their voices pitifully weak and ineffective in their state legislatures.

While the yeoman class did enjoy the freedom and independence of freeholders possessing enough land for a comfortable living, it was not as articulate or influential a part of the Southern social hierarchy as the numbers and fine personal qualities of yeomen might have warranted. Their submissiveness in social and political affairs, greater than that of their counterparts in other American regions, should probably be attributed primarily to their increasing cultural isolation and to their growing inequalities of opportunity born of effective planter opposition to property taxes and public schools.

In any case, this abnormal subordination of the Southern agrarian middle class during ante-bellum years freed the planter class from the threat of class pressure from below, strengthened the whole paternalistic pattern, and increasingly caused planters to allow the individualistic element in their outlook to dominate and corrupt the aristocratic ideal.

Reconstruction and its aftermath shook the Southern social structure to its foundations, but the consequent structural changes were modest and put the finishing touches on the already advanced process of corrupting the aristocratic ideal. For all its excesses, the Reconstruction period did temporarily restore to the yeoman farmers an effective voice in democratizing the suffrage, taxation, and education—particularly in the Upper South. In the Deep South, however, this gain was largely offset by the unforeseen effects of the carpet-bag constitutions which, by enfranchising Negroes who usually voted as their former masters dictated, helped to maintain the political power of the Black Belt planters. This outcome was all the more serious because the composition of the planter class was changing in ways conducive to speeding the demise of *noblesse oblige*. So disrupted and near-bankrupt was the condition of Southern agriculture that old planters faithful to the gentler and more humane virtues of the past were joined (or even displaced) by a harder breed of men who rose to the planter ranks by sharp dealing and single-minded aggressiveness without sharing the more ennobling traditions of the ante-bellum ruling class.

Furthermore, the proliferation of common whites in a stagnant agricultural economy was rapidly reducing the land base per Southern farm family. Despite considerable outmigration, the Southeast's population was growing rapidly while its supply of agricultural land was nearly constant. Even the yeoman farmer with enough land for a satisfactory livelihood did not have sufficient land to give his three or four sons a comparable living—a matter of simple arithmetic which the Agrarians have conveniently ignored. Similarly, the many sons of poor whites could be supplied with land only by a substantial reduction in the share of the plantation acreage each was allowed to operate on a crop-share basis. As a result, the average size of farm (whether owner- or tenant-operated) during 1880-1900 alone declined from 188 to 118 acres in Georgia, from 168 to 119 in Virginia, from 143 to 90 in South Carolina, and from 125 to 91 in Tennessee. During the same period, the respective increases in the farm tenancy rate were 45 to 60 percent, 30 to 31 percent, 50 to 61 percent, and 35 to 41 percent. These trends, which continued until 1930, not only reflect the insufficient rate of Southern industrial-urban development but explain in large measure why more and more Southern whites were being forced into direct economic competition with the free Negro.

The plain fact is that the early post-bellum decades saw the rise of a white sharecropper class whose economic and social status was in no wise different (except for race) from that of the Negro. If the landlords took on white tenants (and the cotton-mill owners white workers) when they would have preferred the more docile black labor, they acted according to a paternalism born of racial sympathy and racial pride. The poor white, his former economic independence and freedom from exploitation gone, turned his gratitude toward his white employer and intensified his hatred of the Negro. Unable to do anything about his economic and social plight, it was quite useless for him to develop class awareness except along racial lines. The ante-bellum scale of values which had supported within Southern agriculture a hierarchical status society, far from being overthrown by post-bellum conditions, was thus in some ways strengthened and confirmed.[11]

Contributions and Limitations of the
New Middle Class

THE South which arose from the ashes of war and Reconstruction presented, in its predominant rural sector, a social structure still notable for its extremes. As Robert Hazel said in another connection: "The elements which made the South a region have not, by their nature, demanded qualities of aggressiveness and trail-blazing energy in most areas of activity. . . . Forced by a calamitous history to an artificially arrested and stunted condition, to the curious state of a living anachronism, the South has [presented] . . . a view of the human condition in its extremes: Not simply piety, but fundamental wrath; not poverty alone, but squalor; and not merely the consciousness of history, but the crushing weight of a personal past." [12] In such an environment, it was easy for the extremes of Southern rural society to dominate the course of events, largely untempered by the moderation and constructiveness of the golden mean of a middle-class progressive conservatism. Even so, the long-submerged Southern middle class was not without its influence, in spite of an initial position of subordination and weakness which it only gradually succeeded in overcoming. It is significant that the middle class which emerged in the post-bellum decades derived most of its vigor and strength from its new urban element.

The already numerous rural middle class of yeoman farmers continued to exist and, indeed, enjoyed some important gains in prestige and influence during the Reconstruction period. To some extent, these gains were permanent. But the gains which many of the yeomen saw in the acts of the ephemeral Radical legislatures and the later promises of the Populist Movement—particularly in matters of taxation, public education and services, regulation of

53

trusts and railroads, and monetary and banking policy—were more often only temporary, long delayed, or never realized. The conservative political alliances which produced Southern retrenchment and disenfranchisement nipped in the bud many of the potential social gains which would have strengthened the position of the rural yeomen. The ultimate result was that their voices were either muffled or were diverted by clever political leaders against assorted "menaces" which served only to relieve their pent-up emotions. In the South's post-bellum rural social structure, the yeoman middle class continued therefore to be abnormally subordinate, inarticulate, and ineffective in either recognizing or promoting its own social and economic interests.

It is to the towns of the post-bellum South that we must look for signs of the beginnings of a more effective and vigorous middle class. As little islands of industrialism began to develop in the towns after the Civil War, trade and manufacturing came almost entirely into the hands of new businessmen whose origins were largely from the South's nonslaveholding rural yeomanry and whose spirit, once freed of the restraints of the Southern agrarian society, increasingly resembled that of their counterparts in other regions. If the most successful of these new leaders formed political alliances with the planter class which produced policies inconsistent with their more democratic heritage, others who remained small businessmen were sufficiently independent and vocal to establish the nucleus of a new Southern progressivism. It was this still small but growing *urban* middle class of business and professional men, not their much more numerous agrarian counterparts, which gave promise of vitalizing middle-class interests so that the socio-political influence of the center of the South's social pyramid might finally become commensurate with its relative importance.[13]

While the values of the new urban middle class were more bourgeois than aristocratic, it was largely they who took over the remnants of *noblesse oblige* that still remained, and their self-seeking was much more beneficial to the broader community than was that of the planter class. At least this new urban bourgeoisie was helping to bring about economic and social changes for which the whole depressed Southern region had a crying need, whereas the planter class merely sought to preserve a socio-economically intolerable status quo. Furthermore, in supplying most of the leadership and zeal for better educational opportunities and humanitarian reforms as its power and influence grew, this new urban middle class increasingly accepted a new principle of *bourgeoisie oblige* which was more attractive—and certainly less paternalistic—than its moribund aristocratic equivalent.

Thanks largely to the growing importance of this new urban middle class (and increasingly, under its leadership, even the rural middle class), the Southern social structure certainly has been gradually modified since 1865. Even so, there have been two major rigidifying barriers to the achievement of a regionally integrated social structure as fluid and democratic as the national norm. The first of these barriers has been horizontal, tending to segment Southern society into separate urban and rural compartments. As a result of this horizontal barrier, which has been largely attributable to the inability of Southern industrialization to keep pace with the region's growing oversupply of agricultural manpower, two relatively independent Southern social structures have developed.

Urban society in the South has been at least moderately fluid, increasingly resembling that of other American regions in its top and relatively wide middle strata, but having at the bottom a much greater spread (particularly as the volume of foreign-born immigration into Northern cities slackened) because of the constant influx of unskilled, low-income farm workers from surrounding rural areas. Southern rural society, on the other hand, has been nearly static, continuing to have two major substructures depending upon location. The rural Black Belt society has had very narrow top and middle strata and an extremely broad lower-class base. The rural upland society has by comparison had considerably broader middle strata and a correspondingly narrower but still substantial lower-class base, although its general profile has been somewhat closer to that of the urban social structure than to that of the Black Belt substructure. If the rural Black Belt and upland social substructures are combined, the relative position of the middle class is of course much improved, but in view of the dominant socio-political forces of Southern history it seems more appropriate to consider them as separate substructures.

The second barrier tending to perpetuate a less fluid and democratic Southern social structure has been vertical. This barrier, founded upon race, has prevented most Negroes, whatever their level of ability or skill, from rising above the bottom rung of the social ladder. While the rural-urban barrier to social mobility has been relative, this race barrier has been, on the face of it, absolute. It has had all the earmarks of a caste system more rigid, and far less responsible, than the master-slave relationship of ante-bellum years.

In fact, however, the rural-urban barrier has been the more formidable one. The race barrier has existed in both the rural (principally Black Belt) and the urban social substructures, and even in the latter, most Negroes have been barred from manufacturing and white-collar employment. Nonetheless, while caste lines in the rural Black Belt society have served to save the poverty-drawn faces of lighter hue, the principal socio-economic problem of this area is a more fundamental one than racial prejudice, reflecting the lack of adequate educational and nonfarm job opportunities for the poor of both races. (After all, even in 1950, 66 percent of the South's low-income farmers were white.) As a result, despite the smoke screen of "white supremacy" sentiment which has been strongest here, in reality the rural Black Belt has tended to have a single social substructure (rather than one for each race) in which most whites have shared with Negroes the bottom layer.

In Southern urban society, on the other hand, caste lines have been less tightly drawn, and, given much better educational and employment opportunities, the Negro has been able to rise somewhat on the social scale. Under Southern urban conditions, the

Negro has been more widely separated physically—in terms of residence, employment, and even personal association—from the white than under rural conditions. The urban society has even tended to bifurcate, with separate substructures for Negroes and whites. But, if there has been racial separateness in many urban relationships, at least within their own urban society many Negroes have found it possible to achieve positions of middle-class status—positions which were virtually closed to most whites or Negroes in the parallel rural society.

In the process, Negroes of the urban South have, by their very economic and cultural progress, begun to gain from upper-class whites a new acceptance and respect which tend to undermine the tradition of racial segregation. If lower-class urban whites are giving up their race prejudices less easily, it is because of their recent rural origins * and because of their economic insecurity as their ranks tend to grow through inmigration more rapidly than do their urban employment opportunities. So long as this situation continues, race discrimination in nonfarm employment is almost inevitable. This means that the elimination of white poverty is virtually a prerequisite to the elimination of Negro poverty and the amelioration of many aspects of the race barrier. Thus, the more important problem remains that of integrating the rural and urban societies of the South through an even more rapid rate of regional industrial-urban development. Once the economic causes of the differences in rural and urban social structures are largely removed, the problems of racial integration should also slowly but

* I believe it is significant that, of Tennessee's major cities, Chattanooga appears to rank near the top in the virulence of its race prejudice. This situation seems to fly in the face of Chattanooga's Unionist and carpet-bagger origins until we realize that its rapid industrial growth has attracted many rural white migrants from the adjoining Deep South states. It should also perhaps be noted that, in pressing for racial desegregation, the South's urban middle-class Negroes are placing broader objectives above their own self-interest, since the biracial structure of Southern society actually protects many of them (particularly in teaching and the other professions) from white encroachment.

surely find a solution. Without such rural-urban integration, one of the principal causes of race conflict will continue to exist.

If my analysis is correct, the South's over-all social structure did lose its monolithic character after the Civil War and tended to become segmented into several parallel and rather tenuously interrelated social substructures. The principal factor underlying this segmentation process was Southern industrial growth, which, by creating little urban islands in a vast rural sea, established the nuclei from which a less rigid social structure might at last develop. As these industrial-urban centers grew, a new Southern middle class (primarily white but to a limited extent Negro) was able to emerge and gradually to extend its influence. Even so, it is easy to exaggerate the extent of the post-bellum development of the Southern middle class and the concomitant restructuring of Southern society.

Even before the turn of the present century, it was quite fashionable to hail the rise of the middle class, and later historians of this period have frequently overestimated the extent and character of Southern industrialization and its influence on the Southern social structure. Woodward was undoubtedly correct in challenging the statement of Broadus and George Mitchell that during the last two decades of the nineteenth century there "arrived nearly overnight an Industrial Revolution as swift and vigorous as that of England." But it seems to me that Woodward still seriously overstated his case in concluding that despite far less industrialization the South substantially achieved in a much shorter time "The 'victory of the middle classes,' and 'the passing of power from the hands of landowners to manufacturers and merchants,' which required two generations in England." [14]

I believe that the Southern middle class had by 1900-1910 won at most only a partial victory and that even today this class has not reached its full flowering in the South. The reasons are many. First, since only in an urban environment was full victory possible, the glacial slowness of Southern urbanization meant that the region's over-all social structure long continued to be dominated by its much larger and more rigid rural substructure. Second, as we shall see in the next chapter, the South's political structure was in any case such as to maintain disproportionate rural dominance and conservative control (sometimes in alliance with Southern industrialists) by the planter class against the newer urban interests. Third, much of the South's industrial development (particularly in textiles) was semirural in character and carried over many values and many similarities in social structure from the older rural pattern. Even the growth of mill villages into towns of substantial size has not necessarily caused them to change their original character as industrial fiefs.*

Fourth, in the South's moderate-sized industrial towns, the urban middle class has been peculiarly beholden to a few major industrial employers. It has been therefore less independent and articulate than its growing numbers might lead one to expect. Fifth, the Southern middle class has itself been somewhat protected from class pressure from below because of the limited educational opportunities which the abnormally large low-income urban population of rural origins has had. Finally, only in the South's larger cities has the middle class had a full opportunity to flourish; but the South has had few large cities and some of its planter-dominated states virtually none.

For such reasons as these, I must conclude that while postbellum Southern industrial-urban development did give the region's middle class the chance to emerge and assert itself for the first time, the resulting more fluid social substructures which increasingly characterized Southern cities have only very gradually lost their position of subordination to the more ancient hierarchical status society of the vast rural hinterlands. As Odum once expressed it: "the large number of upper middle class, non-slave-holding white folk . . . constituted the backbone of reconstruction and recovery. Their contributions were definitive in the regional culture. It was

---

* See, for example, "Blackout in Kannapolis," *Time* (June 15, 1959), p. 48. This North Carolina city of 30,000 people is fully owned and dominated in almost feudal fashion by the president of the major textile firm, Cannon Mills.

upon their sturdy character and persistent work that the 'New South' was largely built. . . . This group, however, constricted round about by Negro and tenant, on the one hand, and artificial patterns, on the other, has not been normally articulate." [15]

Had the pace of the South's post-bellum industrial-urban development actually matched that of the earlier Industrial Revolution of England or New England, as Mitchell and Mitchell argued, the Southern middle class would have flowered more profusely on the basis of a rural yeomanry which could have supplied much more good business talent if Southern outlets for that talent had been more plentiful. In the process, those yeomen who remained in agriculture would have found it much easier to make the transition to a larger-scale, higher-income, commercial type of farming. The South's surfeit of underemployed agricultural labor would have been pulled out of agriculture so rapidly that the planter class would have been forced to face change squarely—either by raising the very low productivity of its workers through the adoption of more efficient farming techniques or by turning its capital from agriculture to the development of additional industrial enterprises— as a matter of simple survival.* Finally, the vast numbers of poor

* The interrelationships between agricultural and industrial development in eighteenth-century England are worth reviewing in this connection. According to Paul Mantoux's authoritative analysis (*The Industrial Revolution in the Eighteenth Century* [New York, 1927], especially pp. 156, 163, 185, and 187-90), the English aristocracy of the early 1700's became obsessed with a desire for increased wealth in the face of the rapid rise of the hated moneyed men of the banking and trading middle class. Wishing to make their landed wealth (much of it acquired when Henry VIII appropriated vast church properties) yield higher profits, they welcomed the many new ideas on agricultural improvements and "scientific farming" then developing and sought to increase vastly the size of their landholdings. The consequence was a large-scale enclosure movement, backed by acts of an aristocracy-dominated Parliament which almost forcibly consolidated small holdings into much larger landed estates. The result was the rapid decline of the rural yeomanry which Oliver Goldsmith decried in "The Deserted Village"—an episode in the history of English aristocracy which the Southern Agrarians surprisingly ignored.

whites would have improved their income status so much that, the fear of economic competition from the Negro having been removed, one of the principal bases for racial conflict would have disappeared.

Because of the South's laggard industrial-urban development, therefore, strong elements of the region's traditional status society

---

But if English landed wealth thus accumulated, men did not decay, although the resultant hardships for the displaced were many. Moving steadily into the industrial towns, the displaced yeomen and agricultural workers furnished the labor force upon the basis of which the factory system developed. Former yeomen either became wage earners or, if they were fortunate enough to have brought some capital with them, sometimes joined the ranks of the first generation of English manufacturers, not infrequently rising to a position of wealth and influence rivalling that of the landowners who had dispossessed them. While the Industrial Revolution was largely the result rather than the cause of the disappearance of the English yeomanry, it did speed the process by destroying the cottage industries of the countryside. Furthermore, larger-scale agriculture was more efficient and therefore more easily able to feed a rapidly growing industrial population. Thus, English agricultural and industrial development were closely interrelated, having as a common cause the introduction of a new business spirit in which both landowners and industrialists sought the reduction of cost and the increase in profit. Without the concomitant revolutionary rate of industrial development, the English enclosure movement would have had disastrous social consequences. With such a rate, however, economic progress in both agriculture and industry was phenomenally rapid, and the benefits, in the first instance the consequence of outright self-seeking, spread rapidly through the whole English community.

Fears of a parallel Southern enclosure movement, particularly through the effects of mechanization of cotton production, have failed to materialize. Most planters have mechanized only as better economic opportunities elsewhere attracted their workers away, the reduced labor supply raising the wages for those who remained behind. Thus, and fortunately, cotton planters have largely improved their technology in response to a declining labor force rather than, by mechanization, displacing farm workers who have no better employment opportunities. One of the benefits of further Southern industrialization would be to reduce still further the supply of labor available to planters, thereby forcing them to find ways of making their labor force more productive and worth its higher income.

have persisted even to the present day. At the same time, the rigidities and segmentative elements which remain in the Southern social structure have seriously interfered with further regional economic progress.

Economic Effects of a Status Society

WE HAVE seen how the ante-bellum South increasingly hardened into a semifeudal society which rested heavily upon the concept of status or place. During the same period, the rest of America was abolishing the last vestiges of feudalism, moving rapidly from a status society to one based on the concept of free contract. In such a free-contract society, each man, instead of being assigned a fixed and largely predetermined place in the social and economic order, was able to rise as far and as fast as his aspirations, ability, and luck might make possible. To be sure, his gain in opportunity was at first partially offset by a loss of certainty and security; but this radically new, free, and open society produced such quick and plentiful material fruits that few of its members would have willingly returned to the older hierarchical system to which the South still clung. For a time, free contract seemed to give men the freedom to starve rather than to prosper. But the consequent economic revolution also gradually produced a socio-political revolution which guaranteed that the fruits of material progress would be broadly shared and that most of the nation's business enterprise would come to accept a social responsibility which carried with it substantial certainty and security (and essentially middle-class status) to the masses of workers as well.

If the Southern aristocratic society had shown the same dynamism, social responsibility, and flexibility as its English model, the results in terms of economic progress might still have been relatively satisfactory. Instead, Southern society was relatively static, to an increasing extent brutally individualistic, and painfully slow to lose the rigidities of its social order. Of course, the pat Southern explanation for all this points to the Civil War and its vindictive aftermath. But, as modern history has made clear, ignominiously defeated nations have been able to revitalize themselves quickly enough where the dynamism and the will are there. (Admittedly, post-World War II Germany and Japan received a magnanimous assist from the United States Treasury which was far from matched during Reconstruction days.) As an excuse for Southern economic backwardness, the Civil War (like the "Hoover depression") has long since outrun the statute of limitations. Almost a century later, there seems to be more truth in Polk's conclusion that "If Southerners had been industry-minded, they would have promoted industry and become prosperous long ago, instead of sitting back and ascribing all their ills to the outcome at Gettysburg and Appomattox." [16]

Thus, not only did the South become a status society; much worse, it became a relatively static society, uneasy at any sign of change. The result was a state of mind, a personal and general philosophy, which has been both backward-looking and pessimistic. As Walter Sullivan put it: "The Southerner, faced with a questionable future, turns his eyes to the past. For the past, though often painful to recollect, is at least static and sure. . . . Like a character from one of Ernest Hemingway's novels, his hope is not for ultimate earthly victory, but for the dignity that is inherent in the bravery with which the inevitable defeat is faced." If such an outlook has been in part the effect of the South's poverty, it has also been a contributing cause as well. Certainly, so long as "The mind of the Southerner . . . is filled with the pathos of lost time," the way of regional economic progress is bound to be slow and difficult. [17]

Whatever its romantic pretentions, the South's status society largely lost those virtues of *noblesse oblige* which, as a basic ingredient of its original aristocratic ideal, had made its ante-bellum social structure at least tolerable and even rather attractive. Ellington White said, "The South is rightfully proud of its aristocratic heritage, but all too often we forget that aristocracy is a state of mind, a morality, the conditions of which are sacrifice and obligation and a concern for the welfare of others. The aristocratic mind is the mind least of all conscious of class because it is least of all afraid of losing its place in society. That fear belongs to bourgeois morality . . . which views life in terms of rights rather than obligations. . . . If this morality is allowed to maintain its control over the South, the South is doomed." [18] However, I believe that White is too hard on the Southern bourgeoisie. For all their imperfections, the latter have kept alive most of the remnants of *noblesse oblige* which are still extant in the South.

Similarly, for all their latter-day concern for the yeomen and the low-born, the Southern Agrarians showed little awareness of the concept of *noblesse oblige*. Had they left off the sneering second clause, one might find a hint of it in their declaration that "The responsibility of men is for their own welfare and that of their neighbors; not for the hypothetical welfare of some fabulous creature called society." One of their number was more brutally frank in his statement that "The inferior, whether in life or in education, should exist only for the sake of the superior"—a statement which turns *noblesse oblige* topsy-turvy. Given such a perversion of the aristocratic ideal, Odum's appraisal is more understandable, namely, that in the South there was little awareness of the "millions of marginal folk, white and black, [who] had in reality no semblance of equality of opportunity or even of living much above the subsistence level. . . . Most of the prominent folk of industry and farm never recognized the poverty and suffering level of the five million tenant folk. . . . There always would be shiftless poor people. There always had been." [19]

In my own contacts with leaders in the rural South, twenty years later, I have encountered with distressing frequency the same attitude, that their low-income neighbors are poor "only because they deserve to be poor." Such a point of view rationalizes a policy of inaction and obscures the fact that rural poverty is largely the result of a defective organization of economic resources and social relationships which can be ameliorated, to the benefit of the entire nation, only through vigorous public and private policies. How else can one explain the paradox that the Mississippi Delta has some of the world's richest soil but many of the nation's poorest people? How different might have been the South's present level of economic progress, despite all of its legitimate handicaps, had its leaders heeded Clarence H. Poe's warning in 1910 that "the prosperity of every man depends upon the prosperity of the average man! Every man whose earning power is below par . . . is a burden on the community; he drags down the whole level of life, and every other man in the community is poorer by reason of his inefficiency, whether he be white man, or Negro. . . . The law of changeless justice decrees that you must rise or fall, decline or prosper, with your neighbour." [20]

Instead, far too much of the South's leadership has continued to remain in the hands of those whose creed is an extreme and irresponsible individualism, almost utterly devoid of any feelings of social responsibility. Particularly as it has manifested itself in inadequate support for public-school education, this weakness of social responsibility warrants the detailed consideration which I shall give it in Chapter 5. Suffice it to say here that this lack of appreciation of the value, indeed of the essentiality, of substantial public investment in the improvement of the quality, vigor, and productivity of the South's masses of people has seriously impeded the region's economic progress. This is not to deny that in the light of the South's poverty the financing of more adequate public investments in human beings would at best have been difficult. But, as the experience of nineteenth-century Japan clearly demonstrated, even a poor nation whose leadership recognizes the importance of such public investments sufficiently to give them top priority can establish the basis for very rapid economic progress. Surely, poor as it was, the South might have achieved far greater progress if its leadership had been equally farsighted and dedicated.

If the South's politically important planters and industrialists have shown a serious lack of concern for the welfare of the masses, I believe that they have done so far more because of their uncritical acceptance of a traditional status society than because of their selfishness or narrow self-interest. Too many social critics of the South have attacked Southern employers for "exploiting" their labor supply by paying low wages. It is not appropriate to judge such employers by national standards, according to which many of their social and economic relationships with their workers do appear to be exploitative. To judge so ignores the fact that the South's wage rates are low because of a much more fundamental economic factor—a heavily redundant labor supply with extremely poor alternative employment opportunities.

It is unreasonable to expect Southern employers voluntarily to pay higher wages or by minimum-wage laws to force them to, without attacking the basic problem of reducing the region's vast underemployed labor force. Instead of deploring the South's low wage rates on moral grounds as exploitative, it would be far sounder to look upon them as an important economic basis for attracting the additional industry needed to raise them through normal competitive processes toward national wage levels, employing ever larger numbers of Southern workers in the bargain. Policies which will more effectively promote rapid industrial development—or where such is not possible, facilitate human outmigration—are therefore clearly needed in the South.

Even though charges of exploitation against Southern planters and industrialists seem unduly harsh, it is true that they frequently do oppose such policies, in part because they feel a self-interest in perpetuating the plentiful labor supply upon which they have come to depend.* Furthermore, they are not always scrupulous in avoiding an appeal to race prejudice as a means of keeping their white workers in line. However, such behavior illustrates a far more serious problem than mere self-interest, namely, their accept-

* See pp. 124-26.

ance as perfectly normal and natural of a traditional social structure characterized by a very broad base of low-income people. Southern employers constituting as they so often do a major part of their community leadership, their satisfaction with things as they are is a major barrier to further regional economic progress. It is even doubtful whether their attitudes are actually in their own long-run self-interest since, however much they may resist taxation to support public services for their many low-income neighbors, they are usually forced gradually to give ground. As they do, they must carry an increasingly heavy fiscal burden, because the poor, both Negro and white, depend much more upon the public treasury than in their depleted state they are able to contribute to it. If Southern leaders concerned themselves more with raising the socioeconomic status of the low-income masses, they would benefit their entire community—including those engaged in wholesaling, retailing, banking, the service trades, real estate, and the professions—through the consequent increases in incomes and purchasing power. At the same time, they would substantially broaden the local tax base, permitting far better public services on a more efficient basis and thereby paving the way for general community progress in which they would fully share.*

Such views—so commonplace as to be almost taken for granted in other American regions—still are far from winning general acceptance in much of the conservative, backward-looking, individualistic, and inflexible South. As Polk recently wrote: "Even

---

* It is worth noting in this connection my observation that many planters of the Black Belt, after initially viewing with much alarm the rapid depletion of their labor force as the rate of wartime outmigration mounted, discovered to their amazement that, by mechanization and diversification, they were able to make substantially higher incomes with a far smaller labor force. As a result, many of them tore down their empty sharecropper cabins for fear that they might later face some moral pressure to take their old croppers back for paternalistic reasons, thereby returning to the once-hallowed but now recognizably less efficient system of the past.

today feudalism is more congenial than industrialism to a good deal of the South which has not yet moved all the way from status to contract. This is the South which not only likes the Negro 'in his place' but likes every man in his place and thinks there is a certain place providentially provided for him. To this South, industrialization, with its shift from status to contract and its creation of a new-rich, rootless and pushing class of people, is plainly instigated by the devil. The Southern farmer still tends to look on himself as a better and freer man than the mill worker. . . . This attitude, which is common to all classes of Southern society, is one of the brakes on the Southern transition from an agrarian toward an industrial economy." *

To be sure, the South has been industrializing and in the process has been undermining its traditional status society. With increasing urbanization, the South is at last giving its vigorous and hard-working middle class an opportunity to emerge from the subordinate position it held in the hidebound rural society. Nevertheless, if the Southern social structure is less rigid than it once was, it must become even more flexible if the region is to attain an optimum rate of economic progress. The Southern labor force still reflects the underlying status society from which it springs, divided as it is into a number of relatively independent "non-competing groups." Whether separated according to lines of race, class, or place of residence, such non-competing groups result in a segmented labor force which is not conducive to the achievement of maximum industrial efficiency or personal incentives.

---

* William T. Polk, *Southern Accent: From Uncle Remus to Oak Ridge* (New York, 1953), pp. 244-45. It should perhaps be added that in Southern industrial relations strong elements of status-conscious paternalism are frequently alloyed with an extreme spirit of free contract (particularly manifested in anti-unionism) reminiscent of the early days of the English and American industrial revolutions. However, I do not consider that a serious problem, since it reflects an early stage of Southern industrialization which will undoubtedly largely vanish as the region reaches industrial maturity.

The Rigidity of the Social Structure

Perhaps one of the greatest assets in the development of the matchless American industrial system was the increasing homogeneity of its workers, reflecting particularly the relative equality of opportunity both educational and economic and the relative unimportance of personal attributes not directly related to doing well the job at hand. In recent decades, of course, the rapidly growing national labor unions—with their increasingly elaborate rules of seniority, feather-bedding, job security, closed shop, entrance requirements, and the like—have tended to introduce new non-competing groups into the American industrial scene. Whatever their other merits, unions have thereby erected new barriers to labor mobility which have not only at times interfered with productive efficiency but have forced American industry to reward workers of equal merit unequally. More important, as the requisite skills for industrial employment have increased, these barriers have placed late-coming Southern migrants—already handicapped by less adequate education and training—at an even greater disadvantage in finding and holding industrial jobs.

If the economies of other American regions are now perhaps sufficiently mature and financially strong to take the creation of these new non-competing groups in their stride, the South clearly is not. Instead, the South already faces enough problems in achieving optimum industrial development without substituting for, or even superimposing upon, these undesirable effects of unionism additional non-competing groups of its own making. The South must at last extend full equality of opportunity—particularly through general education, public health, and vocational training—to all of its people regardless of class, color, or location. Only thus will most of them be able to better themselves either within or beyond the Southern region, thereby destroying the remaining vestiges of the South's traditional status society. It also means that the South's upper-class whites will have to resume their traditional leadership role in order to minimize racial violence.

Given the South's social structure with its extremely large numbers of poor lower-class Negroes and whites, it is easy enough to understand why many of the region's lower-class whites remain so ready to lend support to racial violence. Their general social and economic frustration has made of the Negro a scapegoat—a deplorable situation that I believe only continued regional economic progress can significantly ameliorate. If incipient violence becomes widespread again after so many years of decline, it will seriously impede the further industrial development needed to drain off the race-oriented frustrations of lower-class whites. Surprisingly few upper-class whites in the South have yet recognized this almost self-evident fact. Instead, most of them have condoned the outspoken prejudice of lower-class whites by an acquiescence which means the abandonment of their heavy responsibilities of leadership. Dabbs expressed this problem clearly by observing, "It is customary for middle- and upper-class whites, when faced with the need for racial readjustment, to say: 'We have no great objection ourselves, but the poorer whites wouldn't stand for it: there'd be violence.' The part about violence is always said publicly—just as it [was] said publicly by Governor Faubus of Arkansas . . .—so that the lower-class whites know what is expected of them." [21]

I believe it is significant that wherever state political leadership has taken a firm stand on the side of law and order, as Governor Clement did in Tennessee, violence over school integration has been short-lived and ineffective. Equally significant is the fact that Virginia—which, according to V. O. Key, Jr., has been so thoroughly controlled by a small political oligarchy that "By contrast Mississippi is a hotbed of democracy"—ultimately capitulated on the school issue without even a hint of violence. On the other hand, Arkansas—a state which has been remarkably free of race hysteria but whose politics "is almost devoid of issue other than that of the moment" [22]—was led down a miserable trail of violence by a completely opportunistic governor. The contrast between Arkansas and Virginia is striking. If Virginia represents the South's most status-ridden society, Governor Almond at least exercised a courageous and responsible leadership consistent with the aristocratic ideal, while Governor Faubus' radical and subversive leadership was quite at variance with that ideal. As a consequence, while Little Rock has failed to gain a single new factory since Faubus took his defiant stand, Virginia's industrial development will probably continue apace.

CHAPTER

4

THE UNDEMOCRATIC POLITICAL STRUCTURE

> Democracy is, by the nature of it, a self-cancelling business; and gives in the long run a net result of zero.
>
> —Thomas Carlyle, *Chartism*

WITH its aristocratic social structure, ante-bellum Southern leadership probably found Carlyle's social theories much more congenial than the Benthamite principle of the "greatest good of the greatest number" which Carlyle was reacting against. Certainly, Carlyle's definition of aristocracy as "a corporation of the best, the bravest" was almost tailor-made for the Southerners who rose to political power during 1830-60. In such an environment, it was only natural that Southern political structure and political doctrine reflected the dominant aristocratic principle upon which the Southern social structure came to be based. This does not mean that the yeoman farmers, particularly those of the Southern uplands, ever gave up their struggle against the planters of the Tidewater and Black Belt to mold the political structure and public policies in directions more favorable to their special geographic and class

73

interests. But it does mean that every concession they wrung from their planter-dominated state governments required such prodigious effort that the number of their political victories lagged far behind that of their middle-class counterparts in other regions. In the process of constantly settling for small gains, their independence and class-consciousness were gradually subverted. As a result, having unsuccessfully thrown their limited political weight against proposed secession and war, many yeomen still so respected the right of their aristocratic Confederate captains to command that they responded promptly to the call to arms once the chips were down.

If the politics of Reconstruction, with its overtones of social revolution, gave the yeoman class a chance of achieving greater political power, the effects were ephemeral. With restoration of self-rule to the South, the yeoman's political power was quickly submerged by a conservative coalition of planters and new industrialists, which promoted race consciousness as a weapon against the radical, class-conscious Populist Movement and then under the banner of "white supremacy" consciously disenfranchised many yeomen and poor whites in the process of eliminating the Negro electorate.

By the late 1890's, the Southern political structure was in many ways less democratic than it had been in 1860. The political differences which had divided Southern white men before the war were forced into an artificial unity by a one-party, white Solid South, based on a very narrow electorate which was dominated by the Black Belt planters and, at times, their industrialist allies.

After 1900, political progressivism stirred anew as Southern cities and particularly the urban middle class grew in importance. But the persistent failure of state legislatures to effect reapportionment has tended to maintain a political structure characterized by rural dominance and minority rule over a rapidly growing but increasingly underrepresented urban electorate. Because of these distortions in the Southern political structure, the South has turned toward the rest of the nation a political face which has failed to reflect accurately the extent to which more liberal, progressive, and constructive viewpoints have actually come to prevail. The traditional Southern political structure has therefore become a living anachronism. How did such a situation evolve and what are its implications for regional economic progress? To these questions I now turn.

The Origins of Southern Sectionalism
and States' Rights

BECAUSE of its peculiar economic, social, and political history, the South's relationships with the rest of the United States have represented a blind sectionalism rather than a healthy regionalism. As Odum made abundantly clear, the differences between sectionalism and regionalism are fundamental. His views may be summarized as follows. Regionalism puts the nation first, with the national culture and welfare the final arbiter, while sectionalism gives the region and its cultural complex priority over the nation. Regionalism envisages the region as a component and constituent part of the larger national culture, while sectionalism emphasizes state sovereignties, local loyalties, and confederation of the parts against the whole. Regionalism looks upon regional cultures as the base but not the final stage of an evolving national culture, whereas sectionalism represents a cultural inbreeding interested only in home stocks and home cultures. Regionalism is more receptive to the designed and planned society than sectionalism, which is the group correspondent of individualism. Finally, in its separatist tendencies, sectionalism has its counterpart in "an inevitable coercive federalism, which is contrary to the stated ideals of American democracy." *

* Howard W. Odum, *Southern Regions of the United States* (Chapel Hill, 1936), pp. 253-59. To the sectionalist, therefore, the epithet "traitor to the South" seems wholly appropriate for the Southerner whose value system is first American, hence only subordinately Southern.

The political basis for the South's sectionalism antedates the rise of slavery itself as an important national issue. Finding itself a minority section from the nation's early days, the South developed the doctrine of States' Rights as the best way of defending its interests. During the late 1820's, Andrew Jackson himself became a strict constructionist on federal-state relationships in matters of internal improvements. In 1830, his veto message on the Maysville road bill questioned the whole system of internal improvements at federal expense and insisted upon the necessity of a constitutional amendment if the federal government was to finance improvements within the states. Meanwhile, John C. Calhoun of South Carolina had developed the doctrine of nullification, which asserted the right of a state to declare null and void within its borders an act of Congress which it considered unconstitutional. Late in 1832 this doctrine was invoked by South Carolina against the tariff acts of 1828 and 1832. President Jackson promptly issued a strong proclamation denouncing nullification and threatening to enforce the tariff laws by force if necessary. Jackson's firm stand, combined with a new compromise tariff act, caused South Carolina to abandon her extreme position. This severe constitutional crisis—posing as it did Southern planters versus Northern manufacturers—clearly foreshadowed the day when this sectionalism, born of conflicting economic interests and further inflamed by the burgeoning Northern abolitionist movement, could be settled only by force of arms.

During subsequent decades, as slavery became a burning political question, the country undoubtedly suffered from the sheer brilliance with which Calhoun and Webster defined the issues of sectionalism versus union. The unfortunate fact is that each brought to the debate such matchless logic and sharpness of intellect that they hardened the positions of lesser politicians who might otherwise, like Henry Clay, have shown a more compromising bent. Such giants among men resulted in a Congressional leadership too powerful for an unhappy succession of weak presidents to cope with. Particularly during the 1850's, the lack of a president strong enough to achieve an effective and lasting reconciliation of increasingly divergent and extremist points of view made the supreme tragedy of civil war inevitable.

If the magnificent persuasiveness of a Calhoun * appeared to indicate a solidly pro-slavery and anti-unionist South, the appearance was far from an accurate one. Behind the impressive façade of sectional solidarity was a continuing struggle among Southern whites which has been too frequently overlooked. This real and earnest intrasectional political clash pitted the planters of the Tidewater and Black Belt against the yeoman farmers of the Southern uplands. The Southern highlanders wanted public development of waterways, turnpikes, and railroads and improved banking facilities in order to overcome their serious economic isolation; they wanted a new basis of legislative representation in which slaves were no longer counted and reapportionment to reflect the more rapidly growing white population of the upcountry; they wanted to eliminate the property qualifications for voting and for office-holding which discriminated against small farmers; and they wanted *ad valorem* taxation of property (including slaves) in order that the wealthy lowland planters might carry a more equitable share of the tax burden and support the system of free universal public-school education which the highlanders considered essential to their own interests. By 1860, with few exceptions, the upland

---

* Curiously enough, Calhoun was himself an upcountryman of essentially yeoman rather than aristocratic origins. Early in his political career he supported protective tariffs—believing that the South would share in the nation's consequent industrial development—and federal aid for internal improvements. During 1825-32, however, he lost his earlier staunch faith in nationalism and opposed the tariff legislation of that period as contrary to the South's dominantly agricultural interests. After having come to share a belief in strict construction of the Constitution, Calhoun and Jackson acrimoniously parted ways in 1831-32. While their clash over the doctrine of nullification was resolved by compromise, Calhoun henceforth devoted his life to the protection of sectional interests, which increasingly revolved around the slavery issue. Despite his more democratic upcountry heritage and a personally modest and unostentatious life as a country planter, he thus became the spokesman *par excellence* for the agrarian-aristocratic point of view.

yeomen had largely succeeded in eliminating property qualifications and the inclusion of slaves in arriving at apportionment, and
universal white manhood suffrage usually prevailed. But on matters
of internal improvements and banking, taxation, and public schools,
they had won only minor concessions.[1]

Given such severe and largely unfilled political cleavages in the
ante-bellum South, it was only by an extraordinary feat of political
persuasiveness that a relatively small minority—the whites of the
areas of heavy slave population—was able to enlist a vast majority of
slaveless upcountrymen in the ranks of the Gray. The Black Belt
planters did appeal to sectional patriotism against the threat of
external force rather than argue that their slave property should be
defended. But the fact that such an appeal was generally effective
is all the more remarkable since, insofar as they were given an opportunity to express their own preferences politically, the uplanders
cast solid votes against secession and war. As Woodward described
the situation in South Carolina, the upcountry democracy "subordi-
nated its ancient grievances to the common cause and submitted
to the leadership of the low country and the men with the old
names." [2] That this generally happened—the principal exceptions
were northwestern Virginia (subsequently West Virginia) and
East Tennessee—undoubtedly largely reflects the uplanders' lack
of effective indigenous leadership of their own, a situation reflecting
their social and cultural isolation and the absence of economic and
educational opportunities equivalent to those enjoyed by the
wealthy lowland planters. Significantly, East Tennessee did produce such a leader in Andrew Johnson who, in choosing to remain
loyal to the Union, carried his section along with him.*

* A man whose coarseness reflected his humble origins, illiterate until early
adulthood, Andrew Johnson was one of the few true representatives of
yeoman interests to achieve political power in the ante-bellum period. Far
more a democrat than his more revered fellow Tennessean, the squire of
the Hermitage, Johnson was the father of both the Homestead Act and (as
governor) the Tennessee public-school system. He constantly fought for
political reforms which would end the political dominance of the planter

The Undemocratic Political Structure

While the Civil War preserved the Union, it also preserved the South as a nearly separate entity. By winning a war, the North confirmed the South in her old ways and prolonged the conflict. The common experiences of the war and Reconstruction left a far greater degree of Southern unity against the outside world than had previously prevailed and weakened or even eliminated internal differences which had once expressed themselves in sharp political competition. The Radical regimes of the Reconstruction period, whatever their excesses, generally adopted new state constitutions and passed statutes which embodied important social reforms in such fields as property taxation and public-school education. While these reforms were of special benefit to the upcountry yeomen, only in Tennessee (where East Tennessee Unionists were ready to fill the breach) were reforms primarily the product of indigenous white representation. In most other ex-Confederate states, social reforms became associated with the hated rule of Northern carpet-baggers and ignorant ex-slaves, hence were easier to attack once self-rule was restored. Even then, they frequently proved to be too popular to be eliminated by outright amendment and repeal. The new conservative coalitions which came with restoration found it more politic to accomplish much the same end by simply taking a vise-like grip on the public purse-strings and plumping for complete laissez faire.

According to Woodward, the new conservative coalition which

---

class, although he was himself a slaveholder. In 1841-42, as a United States senator, he won Senate approval (by a vote of 17-6) for the establishment of a new state embracing East Tennessee and adjacent parts of Virginia, North Carolina, and Georgia, but the corresponding resolution in the House was rejected 29-41. (Cf. Thomas P. Abernethy, *From Frontier to Plantation in Tennessee* [Chapel Hill, 1932], pp. 310-13, 316-20; S. J. Folmsbee, *Sectionalism and Internal Improvements in Tennessee, 1796-1845*, East Tennessee Historical Society [Knoxville, 1939], pp. 228-29, 266-67; and my article, "Some Foundations of Economic Development in the Upper East Tennessee Valley, 1850-1900," *Journal of Political Economy*, LXIV [1956], 404-5, 409.)

was associated with the resumption of Southern self-rule was dominated by leaders of middle-class, industrial, capitalist outlook rather
than by the members of the ante-bellum planter class who joined
in the coalition. Nevertheless, he does observe that in some states
the disproportionate voting strength of the Black Belt—reinforced
by the ability of the planters to deliver the votes of their Negro
croppers *en bloc*—gave the landed interests a significant veto power.
In any case, both elements of the Southern conservative coalition
gained substantially from the means by which the impasse of the
disputed Tilden-Hayes election of 1876 was resolved. In order to
gain the conservatives' support for his claims to the presidency,
Hayes—the dominant element of whose party had meanwhile finally
lost its flavor of abolitionist and economic radicalism—decided to
abandon the carpet-baggers and shift the appeal of his party from a
platform of radical equalitarianism for the manumitted slaves to
one which found common ground with Southern planters and
townsmen schooled in the old-line Whig conservatism. He also
promised generous subsidies from the federal treasury for harbor
improvement, flood control, railroad construction, and other Southern projects which Northern Democrats had refused to back. The
result was an alliance between Southern and Eastern (initially
Republican but soon Democratic) conservatives by which the
Southerners gained laissez faire on matters of race (subsumed under
the slogan of States' Rights) as their *quid pro quo* for laissez faire
on matters of business and finance—no great sacrifice since the
industrialist element of the Southern coalition wanted business freedom anyway.[3]

Had this conservative coalition remained unchallenged in the
South, the worst excesses of race prejudice might never have developed. The conservatives did find it expedient to keep alive the
memory of Negro and foreign rule as the only reliable basis for
maintaining one-party white solidarity, since almost any other issue
ran the risk of dividing the whites along class lines. But so long as
they looked upon the Negro as a well-controlled ally of conservatism—an alliance further abetted by the Negro's growing conscious-

ness of the threat of lower-class white race hatred born of a fear of economic and social leveling—the conservatives neither favored Negro disenfranchisement nor contributed significantly to the stirring up of racial animosities. The sudden upsurge of Southern Populism in the early 1890's changed all this. Here was a new and radical political movement which challenged the conservative coalition head on—demanding an alliance of the South with the agrarian West instead of with the industrial East, appealing to Southern farmers and industrial workers to close ranks for the sake of their common class interests, and seeking to unite the low-income people of both races for their joint economic betterment. Once again, however, the conservatives proved equal to the occasion. Within a few years, they had successfully turned their moderate doctrine of white solidarity into a vicious and all-powerful sectional tenet of white supremacy. The far less democratic political structure which quickly emerged was based on the over-riding ends of assuring internally the political subordination of the Negro and much of the white population and blocking externally the threat of outside interference with these local arrangements.[4]

In this manner the South, which certainly had political and economic grievances enough to justify its ancient feelings of sectionalism, undermined much of the basis upon which it might ultimately have won the outside sympathy and assistance needed to remedy its grievances. It did so not only by making the brutalizing objective of white supremacy a first principle, thereby defying traditional American standards of elemental decency and fair play; it also forced itself back into the suffocating confines of its anachronistic States' Rights doctrine which, if useful in preventing outside interference with its rigid socio-political arrangements, seriously hampered its ability to obtain (or even its willingness to seek) much-needed outside economic aid. The consequence, as Walter Sullivan expressed it, has been that: "Decade after decade, the South remains embattled; and through the years, battle after battle is lost. Pragmatically incompetent by nature, and forced by her more clever adversaries into fighting her battles almost solely in terms of issues on which her position is weakest—for example, the race question . . .—the South comes again and again to discomfort if not to grief. . . . The result is a spiritually integrated, philosophically homogeneous society in which public and private feeling, public and private duty coincide." [5] How was such a monolithic political structure, with the single-minded and supreme objective of maintaining white supremacy at any cost, brought about?

The Triumph of White Supremacy and Disenfranchisement

LIKE the fireworks on the Fourth of July, Southern Populism waxed brightly for a few moments and then as quickly faded away. In a South which for a generation had been nurtured on a diet of political romanticism, had substituted race consciousness for class consciousness, and had achieved the unnatural unity of a politically intolerant one-party system, the sudden burgeoning of Populism was as remarkable as its quick demise was inevitable. Though extremely ephemeral as a political movement, it had lasting repercussions on the Southern political structure. In seeking new combinations and alliances along regional, class, and racial lines, the Southern Populists threatened to reopen the political cleavages of ante-bellum days between the upcountry yeomen and the lowland planters, to overthrow the ultra-conservative economic policies and interregional alliances of the planter-industrialist coalition, and, above all, by splitting Southern whites into two parties to give the Negroes the political balance of power. Despite the fact that the Negroes for the most part faithfully followed their landlords' instructions to vote against the Populists, the plantation counties quickly raised a deafening hue and cry about the clear and present danger to white supremacy which a Negro electorate now entailed. As a consequence, whereas only Mississippi had accomplished disenfranchisement before the outbreak of the Populist revolt, within a little more than a decade virtually every other Southern state had followed suit.[6]

That the Black Belt whites and their conservative allies of the towns were able to turn an upsurge of agrarian radicalism to their own advantage reflects the fact that they did succeed in recruiting some upcountry support for Negro disenfranchisement by campaigns in which race hatred and suspicion were whipped up to a dangerous pitch. An upper-class leadership which had long exercised a responsible restraining influence on the natural race jealousies of the disadvantaged lower-class whites now actively fanned the fires of passion under the subversive banner of white supremacy. Failing to heed Lord Byron's *caveat* that "The hand that kindles cannot quench the flame," they created the basis for a serious deterioration of race relations. The consequences, according to Edgar Gardner Murphy, were that the extremists proceeded "from an undiscriminating attack upon the Negro's ballot to a like attack on his schools, his labor, his life" and ended by preaching an "all-absorbing autocracy of race." [7]

Considering how low they were willing to stoop to conquer, the Black Belt whites won much less support from their upcountrymen than they might reasonably have expected. Many upland yeomen had more than a sneaking suspicion that the Black Belt was appealing for support of Negro disenfranchisement as a *sub rosa* device for an extensive curtailment of the upland white electorate. And well they might have suspected, since the lowland planters had their own home districts well under control, having already found effective means of discouraging their Negro croppers from voting or of voting them *en bloc* for the conservative cause, as the occasion demanded. (Cotton-mill owners frequently showed comparable "organizational" skill in controlling the votes of their white millhands.) And, if worst came to worst, their control of the local election machinery assured them of the ability to come up with the right count, however the ballots had been marked.

In fact, in South Carolina and Georgia—the only states in which Radical leaders sponsored disenfranchisement—the demonstrated ability of the planter classes to deliver the Negro vote for conservative candidates was a major cause of Radical support for elimination of the Negro electorate. More generally, the disenfranchisement movement was sponsored by Black Belt leadership which, whether or not it consciously intended to disenfranchise lesser whites, certainly was not much disturbed by the possibility, or later by the actuality, of such an outcome.*

As has so often been the case in such matters, Mississippi set the patterns which most other Southern states later followed in effectuating disenfranchisement. The Black Belt leaders of the Mississippi convention of 1890 won the support of the delegates from the upland white counties for disenfranchisement by yielding on the creation of additional upland representation in the state legislature. However, on balance, the upcountrymen lost greatly from the compromise, which "actually perpetuated and solidified the power of the Black-Belt oligarchy" and, because it disenfranchised thousands of whites along with the blacks, "delivered a large majority of whites into the control of a minority of their own race in the black counties." Despite repeated assurances that no white man would be disenfranchised by poll taxes and literacy tests and despite the provision of a loophole through the subjective "understanding" clause by which election officials might in practice take color into account, it is clear that many Black Belt sponsors of disenfranchisement "saw in it an opportunity to establish in power 'the intelligence and wealth of the South,' which would, of course, 'govern in the interest of all classes.'" Significantly, faced with an almost solidly hostile press, the Mississippi conven-

---

* Key, *Southern Politics*, pp. 549-50, 553. On the matter of Radical sponsorship, Woodward (*Origins of the New South*, p. 323) also points out that increasingly the Populists "favored disfranchisement in the belief that once the Negro was removed from politics, white men could divide, one-party domination would cease, and the way would lie open for white radicalism."

tion refused, despite prevailing practice, to submit the new constitution to the electorate for ratification; instead they merely proclaimed it the law of the land.[8]

Almost every other Southern state ultimately followed the Mississippi precedent, with disenfranchisement leaders seeking upland white support by promises to redress gross inequalities of representation and sectional economic grievances; by accepting escape clauses (e.g., "understanding" and "grandfather" provisions) to appease fears of white disenfranchisement from the property and literacy tests; and by successfully avoiding ratification of the constitutional changes by popular vote. Only in Alabama was an exception made to the general practice of avoiding a referendum, and there the upland counties roundly rejected the proposed new constitution, while "the black counties carried it by majorities often exceeding the white voting population." Alarmed by the Alabama experience, the Virginia convention decided by a small majority not to submit the disenfranchising new constitution to popular referendum. It thereby flaunted the solemn pledge which the general assembly had made in order to gain (after two previous attempts had failed) the popular consent upon which its authority rested.[9]

Only by such ruthless and undemocratic methods was a small minority of Black Belt planters, who were almost wholly out of touch with the liberalizing and moderating influences of the modern world, able to mold a new political structure which, as Key expressed it, "managed to subordinate the entire South to the service of their peculiar local needs." Not hesitating to appeal to the basest passions of poor and ignorant men, they finally gave the stamp of upper-class approval to the virus of race hatred which was already endemic among lower-class whites. When even such appeals did not forestall bitter debate and narrow divisions over the disenfranchisement question, they ran roughshod over those upland whites who rightly viewed their objectives with strong suspicion. Under the guise of white supremacy, they not only put the Negro in his place but relegated most poor whites and many upland yeomen to political oblivion. Such were the forces which were responsible for the South's narrowly based and race-oriented political structure of recent times.

Those who had hoped that removal of the Negro from politics would improve race relations and, by enabling white men once more to divide, would restore to the South a vigorous two-party system were doomed to disappointment. Instead, the Black Belt planters "strengthened their position by forcing the South's attachment to the Democratic party . . . [and] put down for decades the threat of the revival of two-party competition" which would have been fatal to their interests.[10] Furthermore, by removing the threat of insurgency by lower-class whites, disenfranchisement at last gave to the planter class the whiphand it had previously lacked in its increasingly distasteful alliance with Southern industrialists. Planters and industrialists still found much common ground in such objectives as minimizing property taxes and social legislation. But the planters were much freer than before to fall back upon the more ancient anti-industrial, anti-urban, and (as the principal embodiment of these) anti-Northern biases of the more comfortable tradition. In sum, it was finally safe for them to accept a little of the old Populist spirit themselves so long as they could keep it fully under control.

The Narrow Electorate and Rural Dominance

IN VIEW of the history of Southern disenfranchisement just reviewed, it should not be surprising to learn that Southern politics has been characterized by the lowest rates of voter participation in the entire nation. Woodward showed that during 1897-1904 the total number of registered voters in Louisiana dropped by 69 percent, although the size of the white majority increased from 34,000 to 90,000. While the number of registered Negro voters fell by 99 percent, it is worth emphasizing that the number of registered white voters also declined by 44 percent and that of the total reduction in registration 36 percent was white. Woodward also pointed out that between 1892 and 1902 the average number of votes cast for Congressmen declined by 34 percent in North Carolina, by 50 to 60 percent in Tennessee, Virginia, and Alabama, and by 69 to 80 percent in Mississippi, Florida, Arkansas, Louisiana, and Georgia. The participation of Virginia voters in presidential elections was only 10 per thousand population in 1940, for example, as compared with 147 per thousand in 1900. In fact, in 1940, Virginia cast 61,000 fewer votes in the presidential race than it had done in 1888, despite the fact that meanwhile the electorate had been doubled by woman's suffrage and the state's population had increased by 1,000,000.*

According to Key's elaborate analysis of Democratic primaries in the several Southern states during 1920-46, the average percentage of all citizens twenty-one years and over voting in the gubernatorial race—which generally attracted more voters than the race for United States senator—ranged from 12 percent (Virginia) to 34 percent (Louisiana), with a median of 23 percent, as compared with 56 percent in New York's general elections. Even after reducing the base to white population twenty-one and over in recognition of general Negro disenfranchisement, Key found that the range was from 15 percent (Virginia) to 56 percent (Mississippi), with a median of 31 percent. Upon the basis of the latter data, he concluded that "in most states of the South the rate

* Woodward, *Origins of the South*, pp. 342-45. The presidential election of 1928, involving as it did the Catholicism of Alfred E. Smith, produced a temporary peak in absolute votes for both Virginia and the South generally which for the first time exceeded levels of 1888-96 (*ibid.*, p. 344; and Rupert B. Vance and Nicholas J. Demerath, editors, *The Urban South* [Chapel Hill, 1954], pp. 239-40).

of participation by whites falls far below the rates for the total voting population in two-party states." [11]

While such low voter-participation rates in the South have been partly due to restrictions on the suffrage which have limited the election turnout not only of most Negroes but many whites, Key makes clear that the low participation by whites is also substantially attributable to an apathy born of a one-party system and their generally low educational and income status. Because of the one-party South's inert role in presidential politics, neither major national party has much incentive to provide the South with the outside financial and organizational help needed to establish or maintain a genuine competition for political power which would stir up voter interest and bring larger turnouts at the polls. Insulated from the stimulation of national political contests and the debate over great national issues of public policy, Southern politics tends to be factionalistic, turning on personalities rather than issues. With the lack of issues in most state contests, lower-income whites, both urban and rural, display a vast indifference to the outcome. [12]

Key found the highest voter-participation rates among whites in the areas with the largest Negro populations—a fact which he attributes to the superior educational and economic status of Black Belt whites and to their long tradition of cohesion and potency in state politics, relative to rural whites outside of the Black Belt. Furthermore, because Negroes are counted in giving them representation, Black Belt whites are able to achieve in state legislatures, the United States House of Representatives, and party machinery a political potency far in excess of their relative numbers. The consequence of this control by a narrow electorate—dominated by the views and interests of the most prosperous rural landowners—is that politicians have not had to pay much heed to the interests of Negroes or nonvoting low-income whites. Instead, as Ewing and Titus summed up the effects of the twin forces of disenfranchisement and apathy, "the South, from 1900 to the New Deal era, came to be dominated by the upper economic groups." [13]

Given such a narrow electorate, one might have expected fewer demagogues or progressives than the Southern political system has actually produced since 1900. If there have been successful demagogic politicians, it has been because, even with many lower-class whites disenfranchised, the rural white electorate has still included a substantial group receptive to hate-mongering along racial lines. Even conservative upper-class politicians have frequently used the tool of race prejudice as a device to divert attention from their position on economic policies and the identity of their major campaign contributors. However, they have not infrequently met their masters in lesser men who found that the more virulent (and often politically more appealing) strains of racism came more naturally.* The Seventeenth Amendment (1912), providing for the popular election of United States senators, and the increasing practice of nominating by primary rather than by con vention weakened conservative control. Furthermore, the poll tax and the literacy and property tests did not stand up as an absolutely inflexible barrier to the franchise for whites. After all, while progress was painfully slow, increasing numbers of rural whites were becoming literate, were finding it possible to pay the poll tax, and were owners of property of sufficient value (in current inflated dollars) to exceed the minimums established in the aging constitutions. (While the same thing was true of rural Negroes, the white primary long remained and when it was finally overthrown by the courts, intimidation and fraud were still largely effective barriers to the growth of the Negro franchise.) The demagogues always relieved rural boredom with a circus of frenzied campaign oratory, but they also talked, and sometimes even voted for, a line of agrarian-flavored economic progressivism as well. By and large, such demagogues were of rural origin and drew their principal support from the less advantaged rural areas.

While some demagogues were more or less progressive in their politics, by no means were all Southern progressives demagogues.

* Cf. Key's account of Theodore Bilbo's political rout of the highborn Leroy Percy of the Mississippi Delta country and the means by which Bilbo ruled state politics for thirty years (Key, *Southern Politics*, pp. 238-46).

The more dominant, consistent, and responsible elements of the Southern progressive movement were derived largely from the developing urban middle class. During the first decade of the twentieth century, a number of Southern states produced strong governors of a progressive stamp, excepting in most instances the race issue. This new Southern progressivism owed much to Populism but, having lost the latter's agrarian cast and radical edge, no longer frightened away the middle class. Its typical leaders were urban business or professional men rather than farmers, but the latter were attracted by an urban middle-class leadership which attacked the Eastern plutocracy of business and finance. Like its Western counterpart, therefore, Southern progressivism had a significant sectionalistic quality in its emphasis on "foreign" malefactors of great wealth. While Woodrow Wilson appealed primarily to the urban rather than the rural mind in the South, his election in 1912 represented a culminating point of Southern progressivism not again attained until the New Deal era.[14]

It should also be emphasized that Southern urbanization not only encouraged greater political progressivism through the development of a more vocal and vigorous middle class but also created an environment in which the old tools of disenfranchisement were far less effective. Even lower-income people could use their newly gained economic and educational opportunities to circumvent the barriers of poll taxes and literacy and property tests which had been much more difficult to surmount in their places of rural origin. And Negroes, who were flowing into Southern cities in rapidly growing numbers, not only gained the same advantages but found the extralegal pressures against their use of the franchise much weaker and increasingly almost nonexistent. For such reasons, the basis of the electorate, while gradually broadening even in rural areas, was broadening much more rapidly under urban conditions.

With such a new spirit abroad in the South's growing cities, one might have expected a sharp decline in the political influence of the Black Belt areas and of rural interests generally in Southern politics. Unfortunately, during the last half-century such a decline has been very largely frustrated by the general refusal of Southern state legislators to carry out their constitutional duty to reapportion legislative districts in response to differential rural-urban population trends. The consequence has been that in every Southern legislature, there is a "disproportionate representation between rural areas, which everywhere are rapidly losing population, and urban areas, which are everywhere gaining. The South's future, its problems, and its most pressing needs lie in the cities now—yet, as in the classic case of Georgia, where the county unit system gives Atlanta virtually no voice in the legislature, the cities are the orphans of the state government." [15]

The inadequate representation of urban voters in state legislatures (and to a lesser extent, even in the United States House of Representatives) is a national problem, as Michigan's recent fiscal difficulties make evident. But its effects are particularly serious in the South, where the differences between rural and urban interests are sharpest and where rural political dominance has been based upon unusually narrow socio-economic foundations. The population shifts within the several Southern states have been drastic, with out-migration turning many rural districts into rotten boroughs and with industrial development and inmigration accounting for increasingly rapid population growth in the few urban counties. Yet the rural majorities of the state legislatures are in no mood to surrender their preponderant power by reapportioning themselves out of jobs. At the same time, they are indifferent or even downright unsympathetic toward the fundamental problems of urban communities in such fields as housing, sanitation, education, delinquency control, and labor relations. "The natural result of the reapportionment struggle is violation of principles of flexibility, of equality, and even of ethics, to assure continuance of rural dominance." *

* Ewing and Titus in Vance and Demerath, eds., *Urban South*, pp. 234-36. As typical examples of gross inequality of representation, Ewing and Titus offer (pp. 233-34) the following extremes in population per legislative representative: in North Carolina, 5,440 (Camden County) and 51,305 (Guil-

Southern legislatures have thus ignored for many decades the usual provisions of their state constitutions that they shall reapportion after each decennial census, and their failure has survived repeated attacks through the courts. The latter have consistently held that reapportionment is a "political question," thereby refusing to give relief to increasingly underrepresented sectors of the electorate. As a consequence, unless the courts reverse this traditional stand, "there is no opportunity short of revolution for urban populations to achieve equality of representation in their state legislatures." Except in Georgia, urban voters at least have proportional representation in the election of governors and other state officials. But, as Ashmore has observed, the South's better governors are "constantly handicapped and harassed by their legislatures. Indeed, the running conflict between those elected statewide and those who represent local interests has become another symbol of the transition from the Old South to the New." [16]

With state legislation made largely by rural and small-town representatives peculiarly insensitive to the majority will of the state's citizenry, the delegates from the rotten boroughs have frequently proved to be easy prey for bribes and other devices aimed at promoting special-interest legislation or blocking broader social legislation. Such legislators have frequently even openly flaunted their cynical disregard of the public interest by giving lobbyists the complete run of the floor of the legislative chamber. While urban business interests have not always been unfavorable to a

---

ford County); in Georgia, 2,964 (Echols County) and 130,962 (Fulton County). Key (*Southern Politics*, p. 120) also points out the effects of Georgia's county-unit system in the 1946 gubernatorial race in which 14,092 votes were cast per electoral unit accredited to Fulton County as compared with 132 votes cast per electoral unit accredited to Chattahoochee County. In Tennessee, a majority of each house of the state legislature is elected from counties containing less than one-third of the state's population. Little wonder that (*ibid.*, pp. 118-19) "The candidate with the greatest following in the rural areas is almost certainly the winner. Great is the incentive to incite antagonism toward the cities."

legislative system so easily subject to their control, it is clear that the general public interest has too often been almost completely ignored and that rural interests and prejudices, especially on matters of race, have had a weight far in excess of the relative numbers of voters in the rural constituencies.

Socio-Economic Consequences of the Southern Political Structure

THE strongly monolithic tendencies and narrow and inflexible socio-economic foundations of the Southern political structure have seriously restricted the rate of the region's economic progress. Among the more important political impediments to progress have been the South's blind sectionalism; its negative and defensive States' Rights doctrine; its reluctance to give its masses of low-income rural people and its growing urban population an effective political voice; and its consequent perpetuation of political domination by a largely rural minority almost wholly insulated from the liberalizing social forces of industrial-urban development.

Let us look first at the effects of sectionalism and States' Rights. It has become traditional for the South's political and economic leaders to deplore "the disastrous drift toward centralized government." The basis for this tradition is easy enough to understand in the light of a history which very early pitted an agrarian South against an industrial North in a clash of sectional economic interests which both antedated and outlived the embittering issues of slavery. Under such circumstances, as a minority section which was distinctive in both economics and culture, the South seized upon the doctrine of States' Rights as a matter of primitive self-defense. But today, as the South's increasingly industrial economy is evolving an economic structure and economic interests more and more similar to the North's, this broader basis for Southern sectionalism has largely become an anachronism. The South's traditional views on race are also becoming increasingly anachronistic as its industrial-urban development proceeds apace. Nonetheless, the South's outmoded political and economic power structure has become so utterly dependent upon race as the central issue that the region's leaders have kept up the cry of States' Rights primarily as a matter of pure self-interest in preserving their positions of leadership.

This is certainly true of most Southern politicians. Dykeman and Stokely quoted the candid and cynical remark of a Deep South senator famous for his racist views: "Give me another issue I can run on and be sure of winning out in the counties, and I'll drop the nigger question." * For such men, as Dabbs pointed out, "The race issue is central to their existence, for it keeps the South solid and they are the politicians of the Solid South. If it should be resolved, . . . low-income groups, white and Negro, would tend to align themselves with similar groups elsewhere, high-income groups to do likewise. This would destroy the livelihood of the typical Southern politician." [17] In Congress it would also destroy the disproportionate power which the seniority gained from a one-party system gives to the Southern delegations and would force upon them the discipline of greater responsibility, both to the principles of their national political party and to the economically more disadvantaged masses of their own home constituencies.

In recent years, a number of the South's Congressional representatives have for the first time since the Civil War been able "to break through the political limits of their regional background . . .

* Wilma Dykeman and James Stokely, *Neither Black nor White* (New York, 1957), pp. 73-74. It is interesting to note that Tennessee's present governor, Buford Ellington—as Governor Clement's chosen successor—felt it necessary to appeal strongly to race prejudice in the rural areas during his 1958 campaign. Fortunately, during the legislative session of early 1959 he exercised quite moderate leadership. As a result, a wag who had feared the worst was led to comment that "Ellington is not as bad a governor as he *promised* to be!"

[and achieve] national stature." But the recent revival of racism has forced even those promising new leaders either to experience political disaster (as did Representative Brooks Hays) or to go reluctantly along with Southern traditions which effectively remove them from the national political arena. The result is that they once again have been marked with "the parochial brand which cuts them off from the prospect of one day finding a place on a presidential ticket or in a Democratic cabinet." [18] For the South, which contributed so much of the nation's political genius in the earlier days of our republic, this turn of events is not only a personal tragedy for wise and brave individuals but a regional tragedy, both political and economic, for all good Southerners as well.

What is true of Southern politicians is also true of Southern social and economic leaders, many of whom have a strong self-interest in the status quo. That such leaders, who ought to know better, support racism either actively or by default has been explained by Dabbs as follows: "First, being well-placed, they tend to be suspicious of all change. Second, they often profit from racial discrimination. Third, ... though they may be so far above most Negroes as to have no pride of place in regard to them, they do have pride in the place they hold as community leaders. But the main job of the white community, as white, is to keep itself distinguished from the Negro community. Therefore, the main job of these white leaders is to keep unchanged the old distinguishing marks, to stand still racially and see that everybody stands with them." [19]

The consequence, as Key has argued, is that "In the combination of economic conservative and Negro baiter against economic liberal and Negro there occurs a coalition at odds with political folklore about the South. Upper bracket southerners habitually attribute all the trouble with the Negro to the poorer whites. ... but the economic conservatives are by interest thrown on the side of those who wish to maintain discrimination, to keep alive racial antagonisms." [20] More important, by continuing to keep the South on the wrong side of a moral issue which cannot in the long run prevail, such leaders have promoted the very centralism of government which they deplore and have obscured the fact that, the race issue aside, the goal of greater local autonomy has much to recommend it.

If I once took the entire States' Rights doctrine lightly, my observations of the deleterious effects of overcentralized government and apathy of local leadership in other parts of the world have made me become more sympathetic to some of its broader implications.[21] But in the South the dominance of the race question has largely diverted the opposition to centralized government into destructive channels. Dykeman and Stokely have noted the sharp irony of the current situation in which the White Citizens Councils "predicate their appeal on the fact that they are against 'outside' interference, against Federal law which would supersede state law or custom. In their turn, however, the Councils have opposed leaving the decision of desegregation up to the individual communities in these states." [22] Ashmore observed that Governor Faubus, by calling out the militia before the Little Rock schools opened, defied not only the Supreme Court but the locally elected school board, which had labored on a gradual, limited plan of integration which would have aroused no more than a minor incident.[23] The result was not only an official invitation to racial violence but, as a reaction, the "inevitable coercive federalism" which Odum long ago warned was the necessary counterpart of sectionalism.[24] The effects on further industrial development of Arkansas were equally serious.

Even where the race issue has not been directly involved, the Southern opponents of centralized government have sometimes exhibited the same kind of inconsistency. For example, the 1958 referendum on the question of consolidating the City of Nashville and Davidson County into one metropolitan government was defeated despite the nearly unanimous support of most of the local political and economic leadership, including most of the more conservative civic leaders of the community. Even the city's Negro vote, which promised to be substantially diluted by the change, produced a small majority for the proposal. But the heavily financed propaganda promoted by a few of the community's most conservative States' Righters succeeded in winning enough of the outlying county vote to outweigh the large majorities from the city and many of its suburbs. Here we see a paradox in which a few of the community's strongest opponents of centralized government blindly opposed a measure which, by revitalizing and strengthening local government, would have greatly weakened the local need for dependency upon the resources of the federal government. At the same time, by making for more efficient government and more adequate public services, metropolitan government would have made of Nashville a far more attractive city to industrialists seeking new plant sites. Because much of the drift toward centralized government has resulted from the default of state and local government, such anarchistic political inconsistencies must hasten rather than retard the drift. Surely, on other matters as on the Negro question the South has said too much about States' Rights and far too little about states' obligations.

If the South's traditional attitude toward the dominant political issue of race has encouraged the trend toward coercive federalism, it has concurrently impeded the development of a healthy federalism under which the nation's resources could be more fully used to promote greater regional balance in economic development. I have observed abroad that countries characterized by over-centralized governments frequently have also concentrated the benefits of economic development upon a few favored regions.[25] Historically, one could make a good case for the position that the American federal government has tended to neglect the economic development of the Southern region in ways contrary to the general national welfare. In recent decades, however, both Presidents and Congress have generally been more receptive to an appeal for various types of federal aid to the low-income Southern states by which they might close the gap between their laggard economies and the much richer national economy. Under these more favorable circumstances, by insisting upon perpetuating a States' Rights doctrine too narrowly based upon considerations of race, the South has been its own worst enemy in obtaining much-needed and much-deserved federal grants-in-aid for its economic development.

Thus, the South—which Robert Hazel has characterized as being since the Civil War "conspicuously stubborn, sullen, irrational, lethargic, oar-resting"—has continued to "cut off its nose to spite its face." As Lewis Mumford observed, the South has lacked the spiritual vitality of a "soundly bottomed regionalism" which "can achieve cosmopolitan breadth without fear of losing its integrity or virtue." [26] If the South had taken a more positive and constructive approach to the problems of federal aid instead of taking a negative and always defensive tack, it could have promoted not only regional but national welfare and could have won many safeguards for state and local autonomy in the process.

Turning to the effects of the South's narrowly based political structure and its historical domination by a conservative rural minority, we can find wisdom in G. Lowes Dickinson's observation that "All modern societies aim, to this extent at least, at equality, [in] that their tendency, so far as it is conscious and avowed, is not to separate off a privileged class of citizens, set free by the labour of others to live the perfect life, but rather to distribute impartially to all the burdens and advantages of the state, so that every one shall be at once a labourer for himself and a citizen of the state." [27] This excellent statement of the American democratic ideal by inference indicates with remarkable clarity how far the South's socio-political structure has fallen short of measuring up to the standards of modern democratic doctrines. At the same time, the South's privileged classes have largely forgotten the major tenets of the alternative aristocratic ideal which might have made their political rule tolerable or even broadly acceptable. Their power has corrupted them instead, as power usually does. The result has been a widespread lack of equality of opportunity in the South not only for Negroes but for most lower-class whites as well. Discrimination, extending far beyond racial lines, has been across the board—social, political, economic, even psychological and philosophical. And, as Dickinson wrote in another place: "Every kind of discrimination is a protection of the incompetent against the competent, with the result that the motive to become competent is taken away." [28]

The success of the Black Belt planters, who have never been more than a small minority, in converting the entire South to their political will has had lasting consequences. This success has strongly retarded an improvement in the low educational and income status of vast numbers of Southern people, whose apathy born of ignorance and hopelessness has proved a more permanent barrier to their exercise (at best their intelligent exercise) of the franchise than did the old disenfranchisement provisions. It has left such disadvantaged people seriously lacking in the skills and motivations by which they might better themselves economically through migration to nonfarm employment in Southern cities or beyond. It has thereby not only encouraged the use of racial antagonism as a tool for maintaining the status quo but has seriously interfered with the economic progress necessary to eliminate some of the major causes of racism. It has resulted in a rural control of the election machinery which—as the will of the Southern people has changed in response to new conditions and new aspirations—has largely frustrated the ability of Southern politics to reflect the changing economic needs and social attitudes of an increasingly industrial-urban population. It has seriously weakened the state as a viable and popularly responsive political unit and has forced Southern cities to look beyond the state to the federal government as the only remaining source of assistance for solving their serious local economic and social problems.

It is, of course, possible to argue that the South may be able to attract more rather than less industry because of its dominantly conservative, laissez-faire political characteristics. But I believe that such an argument is largely based on false premises. The South's prevalent anti-unionism, its largely submissive labor force, and its extraordinary time lag in enacting social legislation * may have their attractions to a Northern manufacturer who has just finished a bout with a recalcitrant union boss or with a pile of state government report forms. But such factors as these are primarily of value in attracting industries of the less desirable, unstable, low-productivity, low-wage kind which the South's plentiful labor force will probably for some time attract in any case. On the other hand, if the South is to gain the maximum number of plants from the nation's larger, financially stronger, high-wage industries, its political leadership will have to be more farsighted than it has been in the past.

Except where the South has rich sources of raw materials not readily available elsewhere, its success in attracting these more desirable industries depends primarily upon its developing a labor force with or capable of acquiring the necessary industrial skills and upon its having urban communities which are good places in which to live. Such industries either bring their unions with them or at least expect unionism (and social legislation) to come at an early future date. But they also expect a good public school system and adequate public services for both their workers and their imported managerial personnel; they want a community which provides satisfactory streets, sewerage, zoning laws, and police and fire protection; and they require an atmosphere of law and order. Hence, they want more rather than less government and, far from seeking bribes and special concessions, are willing to carry their share of the tax load needed to support it. But they do demand, and properly, that state and local government be responsible and efficient and that tax policy be nondiscriminatory. Since nothing succeeds like success, such industries will be attracted at an accelerating pace as new industrial payrolls raise the purchasing power of the masses, so that the South becomes more important as a market for industrial goods.

* When Mississippi finally joined the rest of the Union in 1948 by enacting a workmen's compensation law, the occasion still aroused extended and bitter debate in the legislature! (Key, *Southern Politics*, p. 241n.)

The Undemocratic Political Structure

With few exceptions, the rurally dominated state legislatures of the South have starved their urban constituencies financially and have refused to extend to them sufficient local autonomy to adjust to these new social and economic needs as they arise. For these reasons, unless the Southern states can find ways of making their anachronistic political structures more democratic, more representative, more responsible, and more flexible, both the rural and the urban South will surely continue to lag seriously behind the rest of the nation in their rate of economic progress.

CHAPTER

5

THE WEAKNESS OF SOCIAL RESPONSIBILITY

Helena. Oft expectation fails, and most oft there
Where most it promises....
— Shakespeare, *All's Well that Ends Well*

IN Chapter 3, I argued at some length that, at its best, the
Southern aristocratic ideal contained a large measure of *noblesse
oblige* which, while promising much, ultimately delivered little.
Perhaps one reason was that, whatever the high-sounding resolu-
tions of the ante-bellum aristocrats, the doctrine of *noblesse oblige*
was never fully developed or institutionalized in the South. Instead,
even in the heyday of aristocratic pretensions, "the idea of social
responsibility which grew up in the South remained always a
narrow and purely personal one." With *noblesse oblige* already
seriously compromised by an extreme individualism inherited from
the frontier, the effects were, in Cash's colorful language, that
"hardly any Southerner of the master class ever . . . concerned himself about the systematic raising of the economic and social level of
[the] masses. And if occasional men . . . kept free schools for their
neighborhoods, these same men would take the lead in indignantly

rejecting the Yankee idea of universal free schools maintained at the public charge—would condemn the run of Southern whites to grow up in illiteracy and animal ignorance in the calm conviction of acting entirely for the public good." [1]

As if such social attitudes were not bad enough, the immediate post-bellum decades saw in the South the almost complete triumph of the most brutal kind of individualism. During this later period, Cash notes that there emerged "a gathering tendency toward a more ruthless enunciation, even by good men, of the old brutal individualistic doctrine ... that every man was, in economics at any rate, absolutely responsible for himself, and that whatever he got in this world was exactly what he deserved." [2] Actually, I believe that the problem ran much deeper than mere economic individualism. It should not be forgotten that the Southern upper classes gave special emphasis to "family," "breeding," and blood-lines, with the implication that superior socio-economic status was simply an index of qualities inherited from biologically superior forebears. If their naïve biological theories seemed to find increasing scientific support in the writings of Darwin and Mendel, the result was false sociological conclusions which enabled the high-born to rationalize their neglect of their lesser neighbors. The argument went thus: since social and economic circumstances are environmental and since environmental changes cannot affect the inborn qualities of succeeding generations, they are not of any real importance.

It is interesting to note that England, whose social structure made it equally ripe for the acceptance of such a biologically based social theory, produced several great economists from Mill to Pigou who rather fully refuted these sociological implications of the laws of heredity. A. C. Pigou, without denying the biological premise, replied that "the environment of one generation *can* produce a lasting result, because it can affect the environment of future generations. Environments, in short, as well as people, have children." While human beings are no less subject to the laws of heredity than animals, the human race differs in having found ways to communicate to its succeeding generations advances in the world of ideas. While each new man must begin biologically where his last ancestor began, each new idea begins where its last ancestor left off. "In this way a . . . progressive change of environment is brought about, and, since environment is admittedly able to exert an important influence on persons actually subjected to it, such a change may produce enduring consequences." *

To those who feared on Darwinian grounds that economic (and associated medical) progress would interfere with a desirable process of biological selection, Pigou replied: "If increased wealth removes influences that make for the elimination of the unfit, it also removes influences that make for the weakening of the fit." Finally, said Pigou, insofar as it is true that poverty and "bad" original qualities are associated, the fear that a redistribution of income in favor of the more fertile poor would dilute the better inborn qualities of mankind by increased numbers from inferior stock was unwarranted in view of the almost universal tendency of men to reduce their reproduction rates as their material well-being improves.[3]

For the post-bellum South, however, it is clear that whether its theoretical basis was social, economic, or biological, the individualism of the dominant class was extreme and socially irresponsible. In no single regard was this weakness of the sentiments of social responsibility so harmful as in the vital realm of public-school education, where the effects have been serious right up to the present date. In recent times, the attitudes of the dominant classes toward industrialization and outmigration also have frequently reflected the same heritage. In the remainder of this chapter, I shall consider

---

* A. C. Pigou, *The Economics of Welfare* (London, 1948), Part I, Chapter X, especially pp. 112-14. For lay readers I should perhaps point out that Pigou was of the great lineage of English economists extending from Adam Smith through John Stuart Mill (and his fellow Benthamites) to Alfred Marshall. In his classic *Principles of Economics* ([London, 1930], pp. 780, 563), Pigou's great teacher Marshall had long before expressed much the same point of view in eloquent terms.

how traditional Southern social attitudes, through their impingement upon the quality of education and the rates of industrial-urban development, have been a serious barrier to regional economic progress.

Indifference and Antagonism to Public Schools

BEFORE the Civil War, the development of public schools languished throughout the South. Here, the experiences of Virginia and Tennessee are probably representative. While Thomas Jefferson had unsuccessfully sought the establishment in Virginia of a tax-supported system of universal common-school education as early as 1779, both state and local support for schools was meager during the ante-bellum years. Public schools were considered primarily as schools for paupers, for the support of which men of property were not disposed to tax themselves. Nonetheless, the smaller farms, less sharp social distinctions, and dearth of good private schools in the western counties of Virginia (including modern West Virginia) made public education a vital sectional issue, culminating in the provision for increased financial support for Virginia's common schools in the constitution of 1851. Even so, during the 1850's public education in Virginia continued to suffer from mismanagement of the state's school funds and their diversion to other uses.[4]

The state of Tennessee entered the Union too early for its schools to benefit significantly from public land policy. By 1806, when provision was at last made by interstate compact for reserving one-sixteenth of all future land grants in Tennessee for the use of schools, little unclaimed land of much agricultural value remained. Subsequent sales of the residual public lands to provide a fund significantly labelled "for the education of the poor" yielded very little revenue. By acts of 1830 and 1838 the legislature sought to supplement the state school fund from non-tax sources, but the fund showed little growth. It was not until 1854 that Governor Andrew Johnson of East Tennessee pushed through the act in which Tennessee imposed her first state taxes and authorized the first county taxes for the support of education. This legislation represented a narrow victory of the yeomanry of East Tennessee over the wealthier planters of the rest of the state. The resulting public schools were still not able to hold their own with the private and denominational schools favored by persons of means.[5]

During the Reconstruction years immediately following the Civil War, both Virginia and Tennessee enacted some much-needed educational reforms which partially survived the later return of the ex-Confederates to political power. In 1869, a carpet-bag constitutional convention in Virginia adopted a new state constitution which provided for the establishment of free schools throughout the state. Under this constitution, the Virginia assembly created in 1870 the first plan of general public education in the state's history and provided for state property taxation and authorized local taxation for school purposes. During the next decade, despite formidable political and financial obstacles, Virginia's public schools made considerable progress but no more than held their own from 1882 until the constitution of 1902 awakened a renewed interest in improving the state's public-school systems.[6]

Meanwhile, educational policy in Tennessee had taken a similar course. In 1867 the radical legislature of Tennessee (which was dominated by East Tennesseans of Union loyalties) enacted the most progressive educational measure in state history, providing a sound financial basis of property and poll taxes for public-school support. With the return of the ex-Confederate Democrats to power in 1869 this act was repealed, and a new act abolishing all supervisory school offices and abandoning all property taxes for schools made all responsibilities for common schools both local and voluntary. The new constitution of 1870 repaired part of this damage and, with the tide for tax-supported, free schools running

too strongly to be curbed, the Democratic legislature of 1873 substantially re-enacted the school law of 1867, which still remains
the parent act for the state's modern public-school system. With
new social forces abroad, public-school legislation at the primary-
school level made steady, if slow, progress in Tennessee for the
rest of the century. However, only after 1906 in Virginia and after
1891 in Tennessee did the complete dominance of private acade-
mies in secondary education begin to be challenged by public
support of high schools as well.[7]

It is also interesting to note that it was 1920 in Tennessee and
1950 in Virginia before public financial support of the public
schools per school child, relative to the national average, surpassed
the relative level each state had already attained in 1850. While
Virginia's relative support of public education has generally exceeded Tennessee's, the latter state recovered its ante-bellum relative level at a somewhat earlier date.* Given the economic dilemma
of high birth rates and generally low incomes which both states
have faced since the Civil War, the extent to which their financial
support of public schools gained on the national average during
1900-1950 represents a considerable achievement. This progress was
made in spite of the constant barrier which the indifference, or
even the outright antagonism, of much of the dominant socio-
economic class in each state offered to the general advancement of
public education. And it is the heritage of this indifference and antagonism toward mass education which continues to handicap the
South's educational progress and therefore its general economic
development even today.

* For Tennessee, the relatives (United States average = 100) were as follows: 47 (1850), 38 (1880), 26 (1900), 49 (1920), and 60 (1950). For Virginia, the corresponding relatives were 69 (1850), 26 (1900), 66 (1920),
54 (1930), and 75 (1950). While it was necessary to change the definition
of the index several times over the century 1850-1950 (Nicholls, "Some
Foundations of Economic Development," Table 12, p. 412), the state and
national indexes were comparable in each given year. It should also be
emphasized that the index for 1850 was per white school child, and from
1880 on, was per school child white or colored.

The Weakness of Social Responsibility

The cause of public education after the Civil War was not without prominent supporters. That Virginia aristocrat and great American, Robert E. Lee, declared that "the thorough education of all classes of people is the most efficacious means for promoting the prosperity of the South." Walter Hines Page wrote in 1896 that "a public-school system generously supported by public sentiment, and generally maintained by both state and local taxation, is the only effective means to develop the forgotten man . . . and the forgotten woman." Nor was the Negro excluded by some, such as Clarence H. Poe, who declared in 1910 that "we must . . . frame a scheme of education and training that will keep [the Negro] from dragging down the whole level of life, that will make him more efficient, a prosperity-maker. . . . We must either have the Negro trained, or we must not have him at all. Untrained he is a burden on us all. . . . Our economic law knows no colour line." Yet a great Southern educator, Edwin Mims, had to note sadly in 1926 that "the Southern States still have a great mass of uneducated people, sensitive, passionate, prejudiced, and another mass of the half-educated who have very little intellectual curiosity or independence of judgment." [8]

If some of the South's intellectual leaders agreed with such indictments of the products of regional education, in doing so they turned their fury on the public schools. Woodward, for example, has shown how the Redeemers—who took over the leadership in state and local government with the restoration of self-rule to the South—took "retrenchment" as their watchword and frankly constituted themselves as the champions of the property owner. In the process, public education, which bore the stigma of carpet-bag sponsorship and raised the unpleasant image of the ubiquitous "horse-faced Yankee schoolma'ams" of the bitter Reconstruction years, was first to suffer. Governor Holliday of Virginia considered public schools "a luxury . . . to be paid for like any other luxury, by the people who wish their benefits." And the editor and counsel for Virginia state-bondholders, William L. Royall, declared that free education beyond the barest rudiments was "imported here by a gang of carpetbaggers"; that taxation in its support was socialistic; and that it should be provided only for pauper children as before the war. Great as was the South's poverty, Woodward observed, "poverty can not explain away the shortcomings of Redemption. Measured in terms of ignorance and suffering the results of the Redeemers' neglect of social responsibilities were grave. Perhaps a more permanent injury was the set of values imposed upon the Southern mind by the rationalization of this negligence." *

If the advocates of mass education little more than held their own against their opponents up to 1900, that year marked an important turning point. With the assistance of Northern philanthropy, zealous and highminded Southerners—most of them urban middle-class professional people—began an educational crusade which met with considerable success, particularly in the Upper South. North Carolina furnished much of the intellectual leadership (Page, Poe, Alderman, McIver) and the most effective political leader, Governor Aycock. However, Woodward concluded, "The peculiar Southern combination of poverty, excessive numbers of children over adults, and duplication for two races proved in the end more of a problem than Southern resources, philanthropy, and good intentions could solve." [9] In my opinion, Woodward's conclusion for the latter-day failings of Southern educational progress concedes too much, particularly for the richer Black Belt and urban areas of the South. Having admitted that poverty was an inadequate explanation for the educational shortcomings of the prostrate, late nineteenth-century South, he too readily accepts the poverty of a partially recovered South as an excuse for continued shortcomings in the support of education.

The blunt fact is that far too much of the South's conserva-

---

* Woodward, *Origins of the New South*, pp. 61-62. Woodward added (p. 65) that this laissez-faire reaction "was only natural and would have yielded in due time to the pressing needs for government services, regulation, and action had it not happened that at the height of the reaction many states adopted new constitutions that froze a passing mood into fundamental law for decades."

tive socio-political leadership, particularly that important segment rooted in the rural Black Belt,* has remained indifferent or even antagonistic to the whole idea of universal public-school education right up to the present day. Much of that leadership would even today lend a very sympathetic ear to the virulent attack which one of the Vanderbilt Agrarians, John Gould Fletcher, made in 1930

* The United States Bureau of the Census in *Farms and Farm People* (Washington, 1952), Table 14, p. 60, made an interesting cross-classification for 1949 between farms by gross cash farm income and the educational attainment of their farm operators:

Full-time Commercial Farms with Gross Cash Farm Income of	Median Years of School Completed by Farm Operator	
	South	Non-South
$ 250–1,199	6.1	8.3
1,200–2,499	6.8	8.6
2,500–4,999	7.6	8.6
5,000–9,999	8.5	8.8
Over $10,000	10.5	10.2
All-farm Average	7.1	8.7

These figures are revealing on several counts, indicating (1) that the in-equalities of educational opportunity between low-income and high-income farmers are much greater in the South than in the rest of the nation (com-pare the ranges of 6.1-10.5 and 8.3-10.2); (2) that farm operators of any given income class (though the class intervals are admittedly wide) are better educated in other regions than in the South except (3) that the highest-income farm operators of the South are actually somewhat better educated (10.5 years) than their counterparts (10.2 years) in the other American regions!

The South's relatively poorer showing on the first two counts undoubt-edly reflects its educational neglect of rural Negroes (who are largely concentrated in the two lowest-income classes) and its much larger propor-tion of low-income farmers of both races who are unable to contribute much to the educational needs of either their own children or those of their rural communities. But the data do indicate that for their own families if not for their broader communities the highest-income farmers of the South have found the means of overcoming the educational handicaps faced by their numerous low-income neighbors.

upon the very foundations of the public-school concept. Accepting the necessity of schools of some sort for the South—"public schools, if not private schools, on the principle that something is better than nothing"—Fletcher seriously questioned "whether the present-day public-school system in the South is an ally to culture and to civilization." Since the public schools had contributed much to the "industrial degradation" of such places as Lowell, Pittsburgh, and Paterson, the fact that "the public-school system has not taken such a strangle hold on the South ... may be, after all, matter for congratulations." But let Fletcher continue:

> That this system of high-school instruction should have spread to the South from the North, in the wake of Reconstruction, was a disaster of the first magnitude. It was not ... adapted to Southern life, for three reasons. First, our population is still predominantly agricultural and rural. The difficulty of finding capable teachers for rural high schools is admitted ... and what is the good of sending an unspoiled country boy or girl to a city high school ... if ... he or she has to return and unwillingly take up ploughing and washing dishes again? Second, a considerable proportion of our population are negroes ... yet under ... present social and economic conditions ... it is simply a waste of money and effort to send [them] there. Third, our present system ... does not lead anywhere, or help the pupil fulfill any later task in life. ...
>
> The inferior, whether in life or in education, should exist only for the sake of the superior. ... But the present-day system of American popular education ... puts that which is superior—learning, intelligence, scholarship—at the disposal of the inferior. It says in effect that if the pupil acquires an education, he will be better able to feed and clothe his body later. ... Its goal is industry rather than harmonious living, and self-aggrandisement rather than peace with God. That is the indictment against it, and that is what we of the South now have to face.[10]

With such an abysmal lack of social responsibility on the part of much of the South's intellectual leadership, it is little wonder (quite apart from matters of finance) that the region's public-school systems have been so inferior to the rest of the nation's. The continuing acceptance of inherent class distinctions, the persistence of aristocratic conceptions favoring private schools, and the tenacity of the view that state-supported education should be provided only for the poor—all these have seriously hampered the fruitful evolution of the South's public schools. In striking contrast to most of the Middle West, the South has been dominated by power groups who, shunning the public schools in the education of their own children, see little reason to tax themselves in order to finance the education of the less privileged classes of both races.[11]

Nevertheless, these power groups have not been able completely to counteract the increasingly strong socio-political forces pressing for ever-expanding support of the public schools in the South. Despite their delaying tactics, they have gradually (albeit ever-begrudgingly) had to give ground on matters of public finance. But the quality of the public-school systems is as much a function of intelligent leadership as of adequate finances. And the very upper-class groups which might have been most effective in pressing for high-quality instruction in the Southern public schools have, by their preference for private schools, left a vacuum of leadership which the residual constituencies of most public schools are ill-equipped to fill. As Dabbs recently observed, "Having made the Negro thoughtless, improvident, and irresponsible under slavery, we found him so under freedom; and, because we still wanted him to be inferior in order that we might keep him in an inferior place, we were glad, even while complaining, that he was improvident and irresponsible." [12] With very little change of wording, Dabbs's comment would apply with almost equal force to the South's millions of lower-income whites.

By such attitudes, much of the South's upper-class leadership has clearly reflected a traditional set of values which rationalizes negligence of social responsibility. In consequence, the public schools and other public services have severely suffered, perpetuating a situation in which equality of opportunity remains an empty phrase for vast numbers of Southerners of both races.

Economic Aspects of the School-Integration Issue

I BELIEVE that my review of the traditional attitudes of Southern leadership toward the public schools is especially relevant today because of the current controversy over school integration. This review makes clear that many of the angry voices proposing the abolition of public schools as a "solution" to this problem never considered public schools important even before desegregation became a political issue. In the interests of accuracy, however, it should be emphasized that this view has today become largely the residual legacy of a Southern socio-political system which enables the Black Belt planters, and the rural areas generally, to speak with a voice amplified far beyond its natural strength. To be sure, in the South's rapidly growing industrial-urban centers, there are many lower-income whites whose recent rural origins make them ready prey to the rabble-rousing of race extremists. But for the most part the moral, intellectual, political, and business leaders of the Southern cities have clearly recognized that closing the public schools is too high a price to pay for preventing limited school integration. Such leaders are fully capable of working out peaceful solutions to the integration problem, given state political leadership which will stand firmly for law and order and state legislation which will grant their cities a proper measure of local autonomy.

As the contrasting experiences of Tennessee and Arkansas have made painfully clear, the directions set by state leadership are of paramount importance. The courage and firmness with which Governor Clement and Mayor West dealt with the initial disorders at Clinton and Nashville, respectively, set for Tennessee a pattern the wisdom of which was fully confirmed by the subsequent unhappy events in Little Rock under Governor Faubus' subversive leadership. Backed by the knowledge that Governor Clement would enforce law and order if need be, Nashville's mayor and police chief had sufficient local autonomy to bring a potentially serious situation quickly under control, with the result that the city school board's moderate and gradual program of integration was initiated on schedule and has since met no further open resistance. Governor Faubus, on the other hand, just one year later, took an official position which not only openly invited violence and a coercive Federal reaction but which destroyed local autonomy in Little Rock and needlessly aroused racial prejudice and bitterness the poisons from which may last a generation.

The importance of local autonomy cannot be overemphasized, in view of the enormous variation in local conditions within each of the Southern states. Nowhere is this fact better illustrated currently than in Georgia, where the school-integration crisis is now rapidly moving to a head. In demanding the right of local option for the city of Atlanta, Mayor Hartsfield has said, "Let the state give us exactly what they are asking the federal government to do for Georgia. Let the people of Atlanta be the jury to decide the fate of their own schools." Since Georgia's legislature is dominated by rural areas dedicated to perpetuating white supremacy and gives virtually no representation to this remarkably progressive city, such a reasonable request has appeared to be doomed from the outset. When the mayor argued convincingly that "It is now a simple question of whether hundreds of thousands of white Georgia children shall be able to read and write," there was little comfort in Governor Griffin's counterattack that Mayor Hartsfield "cannot throw in the towel for me or any other Georgian." [13] The new governor of Georgia, Ernest Vandiver, appears to be no less adamant, despite the widespread rallying of prominent Atlantans to the defense of the public schools and despite the recent capitulation of Virginia to the federal courts. Thus perilously does the fate of the Georgia public schools hang in the balance.

During Virginia's school crisis in the fall of 1958, Professor Lorin A. Thompson of the University of Virginia issued an analysis of the economic consequences of abandoning public education which should be studied carefully throughout the South. Thompson clearly stated the general social interest in preserving public schools: "Underlying these proposals for the abandonment of public education is a philosophy that education primarily benefits the person receiving it and it is therefore appropriate for the parents of the children being educated to bear the full cost of providing this education.... Such a theory, however, does not recognize the fact that the investment made in children by parents, the community, and other social agencies contributes immediately to the benefit of those who employ them and to the locality as a whole in all of its activities.... The benefits or the deficiencies of education thus become widely diffused throughout the entire social fabric." *

For those inclined to dismiss lightly the social philosophy of a college professor, particularly one whose ideas are so uncongenial with a major Southern tradition, Thompson put his principal emphasis upon the pocketbook arguments for which there are more receptive ears in today's industrializing South. Said Thompson, "Abandonment or weakening of public education over a period of five to ten years would undermine the present economic strength of the state." Among the consequences he listed financial problems sufficiently serious to destroy "local government in Virginia as we now know it"; a wholesale exodus of teachers to other states; a flight of persons engaged in manufacturing, business, and the professions to other states "which offer attractive facilities for the public education of their children"; and a halt to future economic development "if the social, economic and political policies of the state are such as to discourage people from remaining ... or settling in Virginia."

* Lorin A. Thompson, "Some Economic Aspects of Virginia's Current Educational Crisis" (Charlottesville, Va., undated) (processed). The reader will find it of interest to compare Thompson's opening sentence with the statement of an early post-bellum governor of Virginia quoted on p. 109.

Fortunately, important industrial leaders of Virginia have lent strong support to Thompson's views. A top management official of the General Electric plant in Waynesboro, Louis T. Rader, recently stated, "I am convinced that industrial development of Virginia [requires] ... a strong, effective public-school system. There is no doubt that the education climate and the business climate are interdependent. To this I can attest by my own experience, for I was personally responsible for the selection of Virginia as the location of one of General Electric's new plants." Rader went on to say that a good public-school system is essential in attracting and holding trained engineering and managerial talent; that the children of all Virginia families, regardless of income, must have an equal opportunity to fill such jobs; and that, because of the necessity at best of a much heavier educational tax burden in which industry will expect to share, "the school situation can be the Achilles' heel of Virginia's economy ... if we decide to build still another school system—one of subsidized private schools—on top of our present one." [14]

John P. Fishwick, vice-president of the Norfolk and Western Railway, recently pointed out that Virginia's record in attracting new industry was particularly discouraging in 1958, when it added only 1,663 new industrial jobs while North Carolina was adding 21,758. As a solution, he urged that there "should be a prompt and sound solution to the school situation based on the principle that excellent free public schools will be maintained." [15] The dilemma which Virginia and other states face when they place their public-school systems in jeopardy may also be illustrated by a recent story reported by Ralph McGill. A Northern firm locating a plant had narrowed its choice down to Alabama and North Carolina. Having tentatively decided on Alabama, its officials visited Governor Patterson to inquire about the schools. The Governor replied vehemently that he would close every one of them before he would accept a federal court order. The businessmen then reconsidered their choice, deciding to visit North Carolina. There Governor Hodges assured them that the schools of North Carolina would not only remain open but would receive increased financial support. He also pointed to North Carolina's great universities and scientific research facilities. Needless to say, North Carolina got the plant.*

Led by a governor with a deep respect for American legal processes, Virginia suddenly ended its mighty campaign of "massive resistance" to the obvious despair of the segregationist leaders of the Deep South. If the subsequent school measures adopted by the Virginia general assembly still permit feudalistic Prince Edward County to stew in its own juice by choosing to close its public schools,† they also grant the local autonomy by which Richmond, Norfolk, and Arlington can make their own independent school arrangements in response to more favorable and moderate circumstances. This is as it should be. If Virginia's capitulation came also in part because of the internal pressures of its business leadership, its decision was undoubtedly speeded not only by the example of moderate North Carolina's recent remarkable economic successes but by the example of unfortunate Arkansas' recent equally remarkable economic failures.

During 1950-57 inclusive, Little Rock gained 40 new industrial plants employing 2,378 people and had major plant expansions accounting for at least 500 new jobs. The year 1957 proved to be Little Rock's best year, with 8 new plants employing 1,002 people. Since the school turmoil of September, 1957, however, not a single

---

* Ralph McGill, column in the *Nashville Tennessean* (March 10, 1959), p. 9. In support of McGill's story, two important Alabama businessmen may be cited. The former chairman of the Birmingham Chamber of Commerce Committee of 100, William P. Engel, stated in 1957 that the unfavorable publicity about the state's racial problems was causing industry to by-pass Alabama, as a result of which "we have lost one major plant in Birmingham and several smaller installations" (*Birmingham Post-Herald*, February 6, 1957). Simultaneously the vice-president in charge of industrial development for the Alabama Power Company, Cooper Green, voiced a similar view, "No industry wants to move into a troubled area" (*ibid.*).

† The obvious glee with which the white citizens of Prince Edward County anticipated the prospect of private schools for whites but no schools for Negroes is socially significant though not commendable.

new plant has located in Little Rock. It is easy to blame this sharp change on the 1957-58 economic recession, although 1958 proved to be North Carolina's best year yet and Little Rock business leaders can cite chapter and verse of plants lost as a result of local school troubles. Among these is Everett Tucker, Jr., who was industrial director of the Little Rock Chamber of Commerce until December, 1958, when significantly he resigned to make a successful race for the city school board, of whose "moderate" faction he has since been the leader. While most business indicators in Little Rock continued to rise during 1958, local business leaders attribute it primarily to the momentum of past expansion which is beginning to slow down.[16]

Frank W. Cantrell, manager of the Arkansas Chamber of Commerce, has also been frank to admit that Little Rock's troubles have seriously affected industrial development in the rest of the state, and the statistics on new plant investment in Arkansas substantiate him beyond any debate—$131,100,000 in 1956; $44,900,000 in 1957; and $25,400,000 in 1958. Since Chamber of Commerce officials are not prone to advertise the fact that their efforts to attract industry are proving unsuccessful, their increasing outspokenness in Arkansas is a good index of their growing feeling of desperation. And despite segregationist threats of boycott which have intimidated many businessmen, local business opinion has given their leaders substantial collective support. For example, in late February, 1959, the Little Rock Chamber of Commerce polled over 1,000 members, of whom 77 percent favored reopening the public high schools even if it meant token racial integration. When the local chapter of the Association of University Women polled all Little Rock retail merchants, all but six reported that they had been hurt. Of the six unharmed, two were transport companies which were moving people out.[17]

Local businessmen took a prominent part in organizing the recall election of May, 1959, which, despite two television appeals by Governor Faubus, eliminated the three segregationists from the Little Rock school board. This led the governor to charge that the "prominent and wealthy leaders" of the city were trying to force integration on Negroes and "the good, honest white people of the middle and lower classes" through a "charge of the Cadillac brigade." One of his business critics, however, undoubtedly had in mind a different Cadillac brigade—that of the governor's principal backers, the Black Belt planters of the Deep South—when he told a reporter privately: "I say to hell with it! Why should Little Rock bleed and die for Memphis and Vicksburg and Montgomery?" [18] Despite Governor Faubus' continued predictions of violence, accompanied by promises not to lift a finger to prevent it, Little Rock's schools were opened in late August, 1959, on essentially the same basis of limited integration as that of two years earlier. Thanks to careful preparation and firm local support of law and order, the school opening was this time uneventful. Meanwhile Little Rock had clearly bled for nothing.

Those who are most stubbornly opposed to integration are, of course, inclined to scoff at my conclusion that conflict over the public schools is seriously handicapping Southern industrial development.* On their side is the recent considerable economic expansion in such diehard states as South Carolina and Mississippi and the rapid industrial growth of such cities as Jackson, Miss. Certainly the statistics do not support the view that there is perfect correlation between moderate school-integration policies and high rates of industrial expansion in the several Southern states. The facts do indicate that particular widely publicized events of race conflict and of threatened or actual school closings have especially serious effects. The tests for South Carolina and Mississippi

---

* Most prominent among the skeptics on this point has been *U.S. News and World Report* (see, for example, its feature story, "In the South: School Problems, But Business Still Expands" [February 20, 1959]). While the *U.S. News* has been almost unique (hence commendable) among the national magazines in presenting the "Southern" point of view at all, it has in my opinion shown shocking biases, in view of its pretensions of objectivity, in presenting only the unfavorable aspects of school-integration experience and in its support of the segregationist, States' Rights position.

lie largely in the future, when the courts force them to follow the Upper South in moving toward the school integration the realities of which they have been able to escape up to now. Mississippi's recent reversion to lynch law can hardly appear to Northern industrialists as compatible with its national advertising appeals, signed by Governor Coleman, to "Know Mississippi: Manpower, Materials, Markets. . . . Every effort is made to operate our State government on such a high plane of service, stability and economy that industrialists can know that Mississippi is a sound, safe and outstanding place in which to locate and operate." [19]

In such matters it is very difficult to get at the evidence, not only because of the reluctance of Southern industrial promoters to admit that the school-integration situation is hurting their efforts but also because national firms do not want to antagonize Southern customers by stating openly that race troubles are responsible for their deciding not to locate a plant in a particular Southern state.* But common sense would appear to be on the side of the executive vice-president of the Baton Rouge Chamber of Commerce who warned that "boycotts, economic reprisals, the possibility of abandoning our public schools, incidents of violence, irresponsible statements—these are new factors which will now be given consideration by industry and business when they consider a Southern location." [20] The widely syndicated business columnist Sylvia Porter recently quoted a partner of the large Fantus Factory Locating Service as saying that at least twenty of its corporate clients were reconsidering their moving plans "in light of the situation in the South." And more recently the well-known economist of the National Industrial Conference Board, Martin R. Gainsbrough, stated that he had sat in on meetings of various companies where

---

* As Cooper Green, vice-president of the Alabama Power Company recently stated to the *Wall Street Journal*, "If any of [our business] prospects are holding back on the integration-segregation issue, I don't think they'd tell us. If the news ever leaked out, it would be very bad publicity for them in the South, where they have customers." (Quoted in *The Nation* [January 4, 1958], p. 3.)

he had "heard them eliminate from further consideration areas which have this school problem, because of the friction involved in them and the difficulty of getting top personnel to move to such places with their children." A Mississippian who was recently president of the United States Chamber of Commerce and an immediate past president of the Georgia Chamber of Commerce have voiced similar sentiments. The increasing difficulty of marketing Southern school bonds, and then only at stiffer interest rates, has also been emphasized by investment bankers.[21]

At every hand, we find that the South's urban-industrial leadership clearly perceives the dangers which recent threats to public education involve for its concurrent industrial promotion campaigns. As Ashmore has observed, these leaders of the New South, "like most of their fellow Southerners, wish the matter of integration would quietly go away, and many of them privately share the views of the [Citizens] Councilmen and the Klux. But they also recognize that sustained racial disorder would be fatal to their effort to lure new industries and new capital from the non-South" and that outright violence and sustained disorder are therefore intolerable.[22] As still other Southern states come to their respective showdowns, it is to be hoped that their choices of policy may be the more judicious as a result of knowledge of the poor decision made in Arkansas. The mayor of Miami has warned: "What happened in Little Rock could happen here. We've got to solve our school problem peacefully. If we don't plan now, we'll have chaos." [23]

Or again, as the attorney general of North Carolina has argued so forcefully:

> In Arkansas, we have had presented to us a view ... of what may happen to people who seek to evade the law of the land. ... Those states which seek to evade have been and will continue to be unsuccessful. ... To avoid the law, the state merely goes out of the business of public education. That day should never come to North Carolina. ... It is unthinkable to me that any people possessed of their senses would say, in effect: "We

will close our schools and let our children grow up in ignorance." ... Our state, despite its great strides in all fields of endeavor, remains too near the bottom in per capita income. To
remedy that condition, our state is making an all-out effort to
attract industry to North Carolina. ... No large businesses will
desire to locate in a state where its employees will not have
available for their children the opportunity to be educated.
When school doors are closed, progress must of necessity ...
come to an end. ...

The most damaging blows yet given to the attempts on the
part of people who, in good faith, seek to keep alive public
education in the South have been given by Orval Faubus of
Arkansas. ... We ..., under our own North Carolina laws, do
not seek to nullify the law of the land, nor to avoid it, nor to
defy it. We simply seek to work out what is best for all of our
people, and, under law, to preserve free public education.[24]

The attorney general here correctly showed that social responsibility is good economics and cried out for all to hear that North
Carolina is a state wholly worthy of industrial expansion. But
perhaps my discussion has given too much weight to the pocketbook case for moderation on the school-integration issue. In line
with the broader thesis of the present chapter, therefore, we might
better conclude with a more humanistic observation from the eloquent Tarheel editor Jonathan Daniels: "the most tragic proposal
ever made in a presumably intelligent land is that the South solve
this great public problem [of school integration] by putting an
end to public education—indeed to all education so far as the overwhelming majority of the people are concerned. ... what they propose should be understood ... as something beyond secession from
the Union. What they urge is secession from civilization." [25]

Rural Attitudes toward Industrialization and Outmigration

DESPITE its substantial economic progress in recent decades, the South still has a per capita income which is only about two-thirds of that of the rest of the nation. It is disturbing that, after closing this income gap sharply during 1929-48, the South's relative gains have been meager in the last decade. The incidence of three economic recessions since 1948, although all were short and mild, has been unduly hard upon the South, because even moderate levels of unemployment and modest drops in the demand for industrial goods are quickly reflected in a slowing down of the outmigration of the South's low-income human resources and the rate of industrial development in the Southern region. Hence, no region has a greater interest in a stable and expanding high-employment national economy than does the South. At the same time, no region has so great an interest in public and private policies which will facilitate industrial development of and (where necessary) outmigration from low-income rural areas. Since the South's urban whites are nearly as well off as urban whites outside the South, the heart of the South's low-income problem, apart from its urban Negroes, is its excessive rural population, both white and Negro. For this reason, local cultural attitudes which impede industrialization and outmigration in the rural South are a serious barrier to economic progress.

Considering the desperation with which most county seat towns in the South appear to be competing for industrial plants, one might at first strongly doubt that any antagonism to industrialization remains even in the most rural areas. Nonetheless, in every such community there are important socio-political leaders who see in both industrialization and outmigration a threat to their traditionally high social status and their economic self-interest. Particularly where the plantation organization of agriculture still prevails, the relatively few but politically powerful large planters see in either outmigration or local industrialization the destruction of the plentiful and cheap farm labor supply which for a century has been the very foundation of their economic existence. Where a rural community has already attracted one or more low-wage plants, its Chamber of Commerce is typically dominated by local industrialists who look upon further industrialization merely as competition which would drive up local industrial wages, and so they drag their feet against efforts to lure other industry into the community. I doubt, however, that such leaders are fully conscious that they are so narrowly pursuing their self-interest. Having known nothing but the "normal" condition of an extremely plentiful labor supply, they are like the typical Englishman of 1901 who when Queen Victoria's sixty-four-year reign ended simply could not imagine that England or the world could survive the destruction of the "normal" condition of a Victoria Regina. In either case, the social effects are the same.

With the dominant leadership of the low-income rural community primarily interested in preserving the status quo, local economic progress is extremely difficult. The undesirable effects of such conscious or subconscious self-interest are compounded by cultural attitudes inherited from the past which offer an easy rationalization of a policy of inaction. Thus, the traditional local leaders commonly confuse community-wide poverty with that of the improvident ne'er-do-well who is occasionally found even in the richest community. Holding a firm belief that their many low-income neighbors, both white and Negro, are innately and inescapably inferior, such leaders find it congenial to say that these neighbors like to hunt and fish anyway or that they are poor only because they deserve to be poor. That better local public schools and other public services, or more efficient social and economic organization of the local economy, might have produced a different result rarely occurs to them. Such socially irresponsible community leaders are frequently not only indifferent to general community improvement but often exert strong political pressures which hamstring the efforts of local representatives of public agencies (such as the agricultural research and extension services and the employment service) to introduce corrective measures.

If the attitudes of many low-income communities are gradually changing, it is because of the increasingly general alarm at the loss of local population by outmigration which, despite inadequate public support, has been at a high rate. Any county which has lost in a decade 15 to 25 percent of its population by outmigration, as have so many of the South's rural counties in recent years, contains bankers, retailers, and other businessmen who face a bleak economic future unless the tide is somehow reversed. It is not surprising that such men have tried, often successfully, to swing local public opinion in the direction of supporting the industrial development of their rural community. Such efforts to reduce outmigration by local industrialization are wholly commendable. But perhaps the most that such low-income rural communities can usually hope to accomplish is to attract some industries which will upgrade local employment and payrolls to a limited extent. Rarely can they realistically expect to eliminate by local effort the need for a continuation of substantial outmigration, although many of them are sure to try. Instead, the most effective approach must be at least state-wide, with the objective of helping a limited number of urban and metropolitan centers to industrialize fast enough to hold much of the population within the state if not within the local community.

At the state level too, most Southerners have quite appropriately viewed with strong misgivings their recent high rates of outmigration. During 1940-50 alone, Arkansas, Mississippi, and Oklahoma lost 17 to 19 percent of their respective populations by net outmigration. The corresponding losses for Georgia, South Carolina, Alabama, Kentucky, and West Virginia were 8 to 12 percent. During the same decade, although Florida, Texas, Virginia, and

Maryland (the last two in part reflecting the suburban growth of Washington, D.C.) gained one million people by net inmigration, eleven other Southern states had net outmigration aggregating 2,600,000 people. Even more serious for the latter states, the net loss was heavily concentrated in the most productive ages, 15 to 44.[26] Except for their adverse age selectivity, such high outmigration rates (if supplemented by a far more adequate supply of farm credit than has yet been forthcoming) can contribute much to the achievement of a larger-scale, higher-productivity, and higher-income organization of Southern agriculture.

But high rates of outmigration alone leave much to be desired if Southern economic development is to be rapid, balanced, and general. By my definition of economic progress as an increase in per capita material well-being, outmigration in and of itself will, by reducing the population denominator of the index, constitute economic progress even if the numerator remains constant. However, the attainment of a satisfactory rate of economic progress will require not only a smaller denominator but a larger numerator, which can come about only as additional capital (both agricultural and industrial) raises the productivity of those workers who remain in the South. In this connection, it is perhaps too much to expect the leaders of Southern rural communities to appreciate the value of regional urbanization to their own long-run interests. It is undoubtedly difficult for them to see that since they are going to lose a majority of their young people anyway, the urbanization of their own states will benefit them too by bringing the economic opportunities for rural youth closer to home. But see it they must if the rural antagonism to urban interests which so dominates Southern political processes is not to continue taking its serious toll on the achievement of optimum urban—and general economic—development.

This leads us to one final important matter. If the South has considered a high rate of white outmigration undesirable, it has increasingly welcomed the substantial outmigration of Negroes. It is true that for the eleven Southern states having net outmigration during 1940-50, just under half of the migrants were Negroes and that for the five Lower South states (Alabama, Georgia, Louisiana, Mississippi, and South Carolina), nearly 80 percent were Negroes.[27] Since the intensity of racial tensions within the South is so highly correlated with the relative importance of Negroes in the total population, this heavy race selectivity of outmigration is by no means a wholly unfavorable factor. But it is probable that within the next generation some of the states of the Deep South are going to realize that they have taken too cavalier an attitude toward the loss in their Negro population.

For the time being, because of the scarcity of nonfarm employment even for whites the five Lower South states can probably tolerate their loss (1940-50) of 5 percent of their white males and some 30 percent of their Negro males in the ages 15 to 44. But the day may come when more credence will have to be given to Secretary of Labor Mitchell's recent warning: "Unless [the South] starts now to train its Negro workers, it is going to find that its possibilities for industrial expansion will be sharply curtailed." Along the same lines, Ashmore has stated that "our labor reservoir is going to run dry one of these days. And when the white labor supply is all used up we'll have to depend upon the Negroes, and we'll find that we've been frittering away an asset as valuable as our water or timber or any other resource." Or, as a Southern professor of business administration said to Dykeman and Stokely, "We're discovering that if the South is to prosper industrially it needs good workers and some of these workers will have to be our Negroes. We also need that increased purchasing power. Keeping the Negro poor, the South has stayed poor." [28]

Admittedly, such warnings about a South with a scarcity of white industrial workers seem to be quite premature. Peculiarly enough, with as high a rate of industrialization in the Lower South as in the Upper South, the problem may come sooner in the Lower South states because of their relatively smaller white population. In any case, the Lower South must face more immediate problems connected with Negro outmigration. In trying to head off school integration, the Lower South states finally made a genuine effort to make a reality the "separate but equal" principle in the education of their Negroes. So long as they had seriously neglected Negro education, the social loss of Negro migrants at the beginning of the most productive years of life was less serious. However, the more nearly the South has equalized its educational expenditures for Negroes and whites, the more closely the social loss of a Negro migrant has approached that of a white. This is all the more true, as Dykeman and Stokely have pointed out, since all too often it is the Negro with the engineering degree who leaves and his idiot or functionally illiterate brother who stays in the South.[29]

Southern leaders have clearly not faced up to the question of how the region's large Negro population will fit into the future industrial-urban New South. Dabbs stated this problem with his usual perceptiveness: "Even while shifting from an agrarian to an industrial order, [the South] has generally thought of the Negro as continuing in the agrarian. Apparently the South has thought it could achieve a balanced economy by letting the whites do the manufacturing and the Negroes do the farming." The South "got the fixed idea that the Negro was not suited for industrial work, and, therefore, in its struggle toward industrialization, it has largely overlooked him." [30] As a result of this attitude, most Southerners have seen little use in increasing public financial support for non-farm vocational training of Negroes who could make use of such training only by migrating to industrial jobs in other regions. Far worse, the leaders of the rural Black Belt communities have reacted to the increasing pressures to integrate their schools by base and vengeful proposals to set up private schools for whites only so that, by closing down the public schools, they can end Negro education entirely.

Little wonder that the Southern Negro, especially the more intelligent and better educated Negro, has been leaving the South in record numbers. Barred from most nearby industrial employment and finding his position in an anachronistic plantation economy increasingly intolerable, he has had no alternative but to migrate to other regions. If the Negro's departure currently appears to be a gain for the South, it will probably not always be so. Here, as elsewhere, the South can persist in its socially irresponsible doctrine of racism only at the ultimate cost of tearing its whole economy down.

CHAPTER

6

CONFORMITY OF THOUGHT
AND BEHAVIOR

> The virtue in most request is conformity. . . . It
> loves not realities and creators, but names and
> customs.
> — Ralph Waldo Emerson, *Self-Reliance*

COMPARED with the people of the mother country, Americans generally have been far less tolerant of men who fail to conform to group patterns and who do not do things as everyone else does them. Thus, as Avery Craven has argued, the spirit of freedom, equality, and individualism of the American frontier was sometimes more apparent than real. The price of survival on the frontier was cooperation, which required conformity in conduct so that each man might know what to expect of the other. To Carl Becker, frontier individualism was that of achievement, not eccentricity; of conformity, not revolt. Frontiersmen tended to be pounded into a common pattern. Their freedom, seldom extending to thinking, was often only a freedom to act as every one else did; their equality, an opportunity to become unequal in the possession of material things, with those falling behind becoming the object not of pity but of condemnation.[1]

131

This is not to deny that the common people of the frontier—through their persistent spirit of protest and revolt against the aristocrats of the East—contributed immeasurably to the development of political and economic democracy in the United States. But in contributing they acted more from interests than ideals and intramurally were more conformist and less tolerant than their aristocratic adversaries of the East. At the same time, the older, intellectually oriented aristocracy of the East was having to give ground before a new, industrially based aristocracy which was more practical and materialistic and which (as the price of achieving the economies of mass production) promoted occupational and educational specialization and consciously developed mass consumers conforming to mass tastes.

But important leavening elements were at work. As the American frontier was pushed westward, its settlers were constantly infused with new blood, new ethnic groups, and new points of view which at least weakened the natural tendencies toward dull uniformity and strait-jacket conformity. Much more important, the Eastern intellectual aristocracy, while steadily losing political and economic power, continued to exert a strong cultural influence. It was this intellectual aristocracy (and the Eastern liberal arts colleges which nurtured it) which kept alive something of the tolerance, catholicity, objectivity, compassion, balance, and wholeness of the ideal gentleman of English tradition. Perhaps most important, this group increasingly attracted many of the sons of the new industrial aristocracy—as it once did the sons of landed wealth—in the process, softening, humanizing, and making more socially responsible and tolerant the culturally ill-famed organization man of more recent times.

Within the South, the initial differences between frontier and Tidewater were very much like those of the North. The Southern frontier tended to turn out men from a common mold which strengthened their conformist tendencies, made them intolerant of those who thought or acted differently, encouraged vigilante justice, and, for the more successful, hardened their contempt for their neighbors who failed to get ahead. It remained for the tolerant and hedonistic Anglican aristocrat of the Tidewater, and his sterner but more genuinely intellectual Presbyterian counterpart in the uplands, to keep alive the love of learning and maintain the gentlemanly ideal. Unfortunately, the Southern frontiersmen were soon outside the mainstreams of American migration and, with their increasing cultural isolation and heavy inbreeding, tended to lose whatever appreciation of book learning they may have started with. When they responded almost en masse to the emotionalism of the great religious revivals of the early nineteenth century led by an uneducated lay ministry, their newly acquired religiosity reinforced their intolerance of dissent and encouraged the view that formal education was inconsistent with either spiritual salvation or physical virility.

Those few frontiersmen who were successful in acquiring sufficient new agrarian wealth to give credence to their more aristocratic pretensions were not inclined to disabuse their many less successful neighbors of their narrow-minded and rigidly intolerant attitudes. In fact, while these new aristocrats retained considerable respect for knowledge for themselves and their children, many of them found comfort in the growing evidence that their lesser neighbors clearly loved ignorance. At the same time, they were too extreme in their individualism and cultural isolation to fill adequately the role of the Cavalier gentleman to which they aspired. Even worse, the older Tidewater aristocrats (and their adjunct liberal arts colleges) were proving to be too inflexible and unadaptable to protect nonconformity and the toleration of dissent. Grossly corrupted by its increasing resort to a defense of slavery (and later to the defense of a nostalgically romantic Old South), the Tidewater's intellectual aristocracy went into a rapid decline, carrying with it the last barriers to a spirit of conformity and intolerance already incipient in the South.

The results of these tendencies were a general intolerance of intellectual progress and the intellectual process, approbation of violence as an ultimate weapon against nonconformist and dissenter, and the stagnation of the South's institutions of higher learning. By thus slamming and barring the door against novelty and innovation, the South also shut out the progressive and experimental spirit which lies at the very heart of a modern industrial society.

The Tradition of Conformity and Violence

PERHAPS the most unfortunate product of the South's peculiar history was its like-mindedness. In Odum's words, "There is the like-mindedness of the region in the politics of the 'Solid South,' in the protestant religion, in matters of racial culture and conflicts, and in state and sectional patriotism, much of it tending to take the form of loyalties to the past and to outmoded patterns rather than faith in the future and confidence in achievement." Too often, this like-mindedness has manifested itself "through attack upon universities and intellectual life; through religious coloring of politics and statescraft; through appeal to sectional patriotism; through intolerance of criticism and opposition; and through continuing emphasis upon racial issues, Nordic superiority, and one hundred per cent Americanism." [2]

How did the South become so like-minded? Even Jeffersonian individualism, with the right of dissent as its keystone, was both proclaimed and watered down on the Southern frontier. In view of Southerners' remarkably homogeneous cultural and ethnic origins and their removal beyond the moderating influences of trade, commerce, industrial-urban development, and later immigrants, it is not surprising that the people of the Southern frontier came to think and act alike. More important, there were soon superimposed upon such beginnings—which by themselves might have given way as they did in other frontier regions—the growing effects of the interworkings between Southern slavery and Yankee abolitionism. As a reaction to this conflict, the South increasingly tended toward an ideal under which dissent and variety were completely suppressed and men became, "in all their attitudes, professions, and actions, virtual replicas of one another."

Conformity and intolerance were never absolute before the Civil War, but Reconstruction and its aftermath finished the job. Thus, said Cash about the post-bellum South, "Tolerance . . . was pretty well extinguished all along the line, and conformity made a nearly universal law. Criticism, analysis, detachment, all those activities and attitudes so necessary to the healthy development of any civilization, every one of them took on the aspect of high and aggravated treason." Reconstruction also reconfirmed and completed the South's truculence toward new ideas from the outside. The result was "a propensity to see in every notion coming out of the North a menace and an abomination; to view every idea originated by the Yankee or bearing the stamp of his acceptance as containing hidden within itself the old implacable will to coerce and destroy; to repudiate him intellectually as passionately as he was repudiated politically." Given this rejection of Yankee thought and the Yankee mind—which is to say of modern thought and the modern mind—the South "established a rule which inevitably crushed whatever tendency to internal [intellectual development which] may have appeared. . . . The result, in a world of poverty and necessary absorption in material problems, was complete stagnation." [3]

Virginia's great novelist, Ellen Glasgow, stated the problem succinctly. "The Southerner learned to read, to write and to preach before he learned to think—there was, indeed, no need for thinking when everybody thought alike, or, rather, when to think differently meant to be ostracized." Dabbs, himself a South Carolinian, similarly noted "the Southerner's tendency to unanalytical thought, impulsive action, and violence," and Woodward, a native of Arkansas, the paradox in "the contrast between the earnestly professed code of shopkeeper decorum and sobriety and the continued adherence to a tradition of violence." [4] In the process, even the Southern gentleman tended to lose the truly intellectual qualities of his forebears, who had loved discussion and argument on the most important social, political, and ethical matters of life and had approached them in a tolerant, nondoctrinaire, well-balanced, and integrated but perceptively critical way. Without these qualities, his continued adherence to the lesser gentlemanly virtues of hospitality, courtesy, gregariousness, and geniality turned the art of good conversation into intellectually superficial and deadening small talk. The old forms remained but the substance of intellectual toughness and vigor was gone.

T. V. Smith has pointed to the paradox "that democracy finds its most stalwart preservers among the aristocratic. In our own history, for example, it was not Thomas Paine or Samuel Adams, the flaming revolutionaries, who preserved us democracy, but George Washington, aristocrat of the land, John Adams, aristocrat of the mind, and Thomas Jefferson, aristocrat of both." If the Old South produced two of these three, the post-bellum South was incapable of producing aristocrats of like stamp who were both nonconformist and tolerant enough to preserve the spirit of true democracy which the masses of lesser men never fully appreciated or observed. Instead, the leadership of the "aristocracy of the mind" passed almost entirely to New England. What post-bellum Southern aristocrat could measure up in stature to the irascible but extremely tolerant latter-day aristocrat, Oliver Wendell Holmes, Jr.? Justice Holmes never doubted for a moment that in the realm of the spiritual, there was a law of nature which established "orders and degrees among the souls of men." Hence, while he fully approved "the democratic feeling which will submit neither to arrogance nor servility," he insisted that free men must also accept the self-discipline of "modesty and reverence" if the excesses of "democratic negation" are to be prevented and democracy is to be transformed into an aristocracy for every citizen.[5]

If Holmes's tolerance toward democratic legislatures was essentially based on his still aristocratic belief in the right of free men to make fools of themselves, his belief in the freedom of dissent—of which he fully availed himself—was almost absolute. Recognizing that the test of tolerance is not what we approve but what we loathe, he had enough reverence for the Bill of Rights and enough modesty about his own conception of truth to be the most tolerant of men. He saw clearly that democracy's greatest danger lay in the intolerance practiced by completely self-righteous men, since "persecution for the expression of opinion seems perfectly logical. If you have no doubt about your premises or your power and want a certain result with all your heart you . . . naturally sweep away all opposition." Holmes the aristocrat might have said of the Southern aristocrat, as he said of William James, that "wishes led him to turn down the lights so as to give miracle a chance." [6]

With the decline in the South's aristocracy of the mind, the best champions of the rights of nonconformity and dissent were gone. In this dim intellectual light, Southern gentlemen set the pattern which became generally accepted by most Southerners: in the world of ideas, one should be easy, pleasant, and agreeable, on the premise that his fellow-conservationalist and he have no differences of opinion and that if some do pop to the surface, they should be glossed over in the interest of courtesy and decorum. Southerners thereby lost their appreciation of the pleasures of debate on the fundamental matters of life and even the fun of intellectual dueling for its own sake. Far worse, the atmosphere of pleasantness in discussion was an increasingly false façade beyond which only the hardy and brash individual might dare to try to penetrate. If such a person should nonetheless "probe to a level where exist the 'realities' upon which all Southerners agree, and indicate a disagreement there, [the Southerner] will quickly become disagreeable. He has never considered the idea that there might be such disagreement, and he has therefore no practice in lifting these realities into the light of reason. Therefore, he becomes disagreeable, and is apt to become violent." [7]

John Hope Franklin has noted that "Violence was inextricably woven into the most fundamental aspects of life in the South and constituted an important phase of the total experience of its people. Far from loathing violence, the man of the South was the product of his experiences as a frontiersman, Indian fighter, slaveholder, self-sufficient yeoman, poor white and Negro. He gladly fought, even if only to preserve his reputation as a fighter." While Southerners have often attributed violence in white people to high spirits and violence in Negroes to low morals, for both races "violence was, and is, a past tradition and a present release." [8] This tradition of private violence was also easily carried over into the realm of public offenses as well. "In this [Southern] world of ineffective social control, the tradition of vigilante action, which normally lives and dies with the frontier, not only survived but grew so steadily that already long before the Civil War and long before hatred for the black man had begun to play any direct part in the pattern ... the South had become peculiarly the home of lynching." [9] With such a background, it is little wonder that the vindictive tyranny of the Reconstruction period brought increasing resort to private justice in which the freed Negro became the scapegoat for the less accessible Yankee.

During the rest of the nineteenth century, as the South's culture became almost absolutely monolithic on the basis of white supremacy, its "nigh-ineradicable hallmarks" became, to Hodding Carter, "a racially based unity, a regional conformity of thought, ... [and] a group willingness to condone almost any means for the accomplishment of the overriding end, which is the maintenance of the white South's re-established political and economic supremacy; and the continuance of a social order resting upon racial separateness." The consequence, said Dykeman and Stokely, was that, "Underneath the pretty legend, the self-deception fostered by segregation became more firmly impacted. ... It not only restricted knowledge, it did something worse—tortured specific areas of the knowledge that was common currency throughout the rest of the civilized world into false patterns and conclusions. Nameless fears became fortified behind barriers no facts could penetrate. The noble meaning of 'tradition' was bastardized to include anything [including the South's own segregation laws] anyone remembered being done for as long as a generation." [10]

The absurd lengths to which conformity on the race issue may be carried was recently illustrated by the furor in the Alabama legislature over a children's book, *The Rabbit's Wedding*, an illustrated story which depicts a white rabbit who marries a black rabbit. A segregationist legislator, unsatisfied when his protests succeeded in removing this "subversive" book from Alabama's open library shelves, declared that the "bunny book" should be burned. The episode had its comic aspect to which the good-humored comment of the author contributed. "I was completely unaware," he confessed, "that animals with white fur . . . were considered blood relations of white human beings." No less than the Massachusetts or Wisconsin legislature, the Alabama legislature is entitled to its quota of fools. But the great tragedy of the episode was buried deep in its news story: "Some legislators objected privately to the restriction, and one even ridiculed it. But they declined to be quoted by name because they said their position might be misconstrued as pro-integration." [11] The extent to which upper-class Southerners have similarly allowed themselves to be intimidated (e.g., the Little Rock bankers who refused to speak out collectively for fear their rural correspondent banks would switch their accounts to Memphis) hardly bespeaks the courage and uprightness of free men!

Strangely enough, in some matters of civil liberties not directly involving the race issue the South has frequently appeared to be more conscious of the Jeffersonian tradition than other regions. For example, a number of Southern state legislatures refused to pass teachers' loyalty oaths when such allegedly more enlightened states as New York and California already had. In fact, Southern legislators had a field day quoting Jefferson and their own state constitutions on the right of revolution. Nor did the virus of McCarthyism find much fertile ground in the South when it was being widely embraced in other parts of the nation, including most of the hyperdemocratic Middle and Far West. If the sanest and most articulate voices remained those of the Eastern intellectual aristocracy, their warnings for a time were little heeded. In the

South, on the other hand, Jeffersonianism seemed to come more from the grass roots. That it did was, of course, consistent with the South's traditional role as a rebel and secessionist.

Wouldn't application of the loosely worded loyalty tests have found a Lee or Jackson "subversive," some asked. To others "the right of revolution" was favorably construed as "the right of secession." By defending the right of dissent and finding the "subversive" stamp repugnant, still other Southerners were in effect reasserting their right to handle the race matter without outside interference. Admitting all this, I found the South an unusually tolerant environment in which to live through most of the decade of anti-Communist hysteria in which McCarthy and his lesser lieutenants of "100 percent Americanism" rode roughshod over civil rights. From this experience I was convinced that, the race issue aside, the South could evince the widest and most genuine support for basic civil rights of all American regions.

Unfortunately, the race issue will not remain aside. With the recent resurgence of racial passions in the South, attempts to legislate uniformity have not been uncommon. The attorney general of Arkansas recently submitted to his state legislature a bill that would make it unlawful for anyone to encourage "non-conformance with the established traditions, customs and usage of the state." State governors in the South have frequently asked for and received dictatorial powers on matters relating to the public schools. The various pro-segregationist organizations of the South have sought to taint school integration with the Communist brush, in the process promoting a general intolerance of nonconformist and unpopular ideas of all kinds. Thus the Jeffersonian tradition of the right of dissent and freedom of thought and expression, in some ways still peculiarly alive in the South, has had to bow before the overriding aim of white supremacy.

Anti-Intellectualism and Higher Education

IN A tradition in which conformity and the rejection of new ideas became dominant values, higher education in the South languished even before the Civil War and almost completely stagnated for many decades thereafter.

As Ronald F. Howell pointed out in a recent essay, "education in the Old South was pre-eminently education for the planter aristocracy.... College days at William and Mary in the eighteenth century were a pleasing interlude for the wealthy, preceding the regimen of agrarian life to which they were committed.... Students were there primarily to refine the social graces befitting their elite station, already introduced to them by their plantation tutors, and to become moderately adept at rational discourse." It was because Jefferson felt that his alma mater had failed to provide a curriculum adequate for the "preparation of good citizens and competent scholars alike" that he founded the University of Virginia, which largely set the directions followed by other Southern colleges up to the Civil War. While the South's institutions of higher learning continued to consider that their principal purpose was the production of the gentleman, this ideal gentleman was still a man of many excellent virtues. As the Southern way of life was increasingly put on the defensive, these virtues began to fade before the prime necessity of teaching "the romantic message of the Old South" and of inspiring "a reminiscent longing for its ways." [12]

With military defeat and Reconstruction, traditional concepts of the objectives of Southern higher education were not immune from attack. General Daniel Harvey Hill of North Carolina argued as early as 1866 that "The old education in the palmy days of the

South gave us orators and statesmen, but did nothing to enrich us, nothing to promote material greatness. . . . [Therefore the South] must abandon the aesthetic and the ornamental for the practical and useful." Nevertheless, "by and large Southern education continued to be culturally associated with the leisure class and pretended to be non-materialistic. To produce the gentleman according to the old model was still, *in theory*, its objective, and the Southern campus his natural habitat." If Southern professors now busied themselves more than ever in lauding the Southern way, their views were now severely adulterated with what Cash has aptly called the "savage ideal"—that is, "the patriotic will to hold rigidly to the ancient pattern, to repudiate innovation and novelty in thought and behavior, whatever came from outside and was felt as belonging to Yankeedom or alien parts." [13]

The savage ideal, born of the awful moment of the South's defeat, was chauvinistic, negative, unbalanced, romantic, discrete, and superficial—in sum, was everything which the gentlemanly ideal of previous Southern tradition was not. It sought, as Howell so effectively expressed it, "To seal off the South as a vacuum package, to reject all that seemed 'alien' or 'subversive,' to despise and fear 'efficiency' and 'newness' and 'industrialism' and 'progress' as diseased imports from the North—these were the sentiments that then permeated the Southern campus, no less than the Southern home, church, courthouse, and marketplace. . . . [Thus] Darwin and Marx and Veblen now rivaled Garrison and Stowe as anathemas to the hide-bound reactionary philosophy of most Southern academicians. But this would not have been the attitude of the cosmopolitan Old South, so sure of its local roots; and complacently to assume and teach this new chauvinism was damningly to corrupt the tradition and pervert the truth." [14] Having closed their minds completely on such parochial issues as race, the faculties and students on most Southern campuses usually closed their minds on every other important and more universal social doctrine as well.

Dabbs expressed the same idea in terms of the South's fear of abstractions. He agreed that the South has been "afraid of abstractions, for one thing, because it had built its life on an abstraction [slavery] it couldn't justify. . . . the South also feared abstractions, certainly theories about the nature of society, because it was too well pleased with the society it had created. Knowing the doubtful base upon which it had built, it feared that investigation might result in disaster—as one fears to probe the damage done by termites lest the house fall down." Slavery having been destroyed, "the white South still saw in the freedman essentially the same image, or abstraction, it had seen in the slave." Since this abstraction, the Negro-as-servant, includes such an important part of Southern life, it is not difficult to see why the white South fears "this basic abstraction, and so, perhaps, . . . abstractions in general." [15]

After founding its society on the "violent abstraction" of slavery, the South desisted from further abstraction while the North never ceased to abstract—that is, it continued to employ intellectual processes as a means of attaining both technological and social progress. As the application of the abstractions of science continually changed the technological basis of their living, Northerners "ended by abstracting the idea of society from all the busy interchange of daily life, and then proceeded to shape the daily life to the idea obtained." In the process, the Yankees not only peddled the "nutmegs" of their industrialism but their sociological *isms* in the South. The consequences, says Dabbs, were that "The nutmegs made the South suspicious, but because it needed the goods it continued to buy. As for the *isms* [humanitarianism, socialism, feminism, abolitionism, radicalism, and in religion the higher criticism and even atheism], however, when the North really got to pushing these partial by-products of [its] industrial movement . . . the South simply refused; she had built her life on one *ism*, the theory of [racism], and she feared properly that any other, however innocent, might end by uprooting that base." [16]

If the South thus accepted the North's economic "imperialism" out of necessity, it resisted to its utmost the cultural imperialism which accompanied it. This would have been all well and good if the South had been prepared to offer something better. Unfortunately, with its general fear of abstractions and its negative and self-defeating savage ideal, the South's intellectual leadership was virtually impotent. Not only had the South become basically anti-intellectual, but this hostility had permeated even into the ivory towers of the better Southern universities. It is little wonder that the savage ideal and its inherent intolerance succeeded—where prevailing unfavorable interregional salary differentials alone would in part have failed—in draining most Southern campuses of their best intellectual talent. If a few brilliant and courageous scholars did remain and speak out, so few Southern colleges upheld them before the terrors of popular opinion that potential heretics seldom got into Southern faculties or when they did they were effectively intimidated into discreet silence. The result was for a time utter stagnation in the natural sciences, in history, in the social sciences, and in religous criticism.

Some progress toward academic freedom (albeit painfully slow) was made after 1900, with the North Carolina triumvirate of Wake Forest, Trinity (later Duke), and the University at Chapel Hill taking a prominent part. Despite its Baptist affiliation, Wake Forest successfully braved the storm which broke when its biology professor and subsequent president, William Louis Poteat, brought Darwinism to the campus two decades before the angry climax of the clash between science and the South's primitive religious fundamentalism at the Dayton, Tenn., "evolution trial" in 1925. By that time, Chancellor Kirkland of Vanderbilt University—which had in the early 1880's dismissed a geology professor for his "scientific atheism" and had severed its connection with Methodism in 1914—could declare: "The answer to the episode at Dayton is the building of new laboratories on the Vanderbilt campus for the teaching of science. . . . The remedy for a narrow sectarianism and a belligerent fundamentalism is the establishment on this campus of a school of religion, illustrating by its methods and in its organization the strength of a common faith and the glory of a universal worship." [17]

Another Methodist institution, Trinity College (Duke), stood its ground in 1903 against strident demands for the dismissal of its history professor, John Spencer Bassett, who had asserted in print that Booker T. Washington was the greatest Southerner of the century save Robert E. Lee. Other Southern professors of history gradually emerged who, despite the occupational hazards of such beliefs, no longer considered that their primary role was simply to propagate the sentimental and romantic legends of the Old South. Even more noteworthy was the return of Howard W. Odum to his native Georgia, followed a few years later by his shift to the University of North Carolina, which gave haven to the first thoroughgoing sociological investigations and analyses of the Southern region. All Southern social scientists owe a great debt to Odum for starting the region's first intellectually respectable social-science research and instruction and to Chapel Hill for providing the protective environment which permitted his (and Rupert Vance's) many iconoclastic findings to see the light of day.

With the South's stubborn embargo against new ideas and the extent to which members of the major fundamentalist and evangelical Protestant sects dominated the governing boards of the South's myriad church-affiliated private colleges and even its public universities, it is perhaps remarkable that the offenses against academic freedom were as few as they were. In spite of their stifling intellectual environment and their meager financial resources, an increasing number of Southern faculties began to welcome and shelter "men who deliberately chose to know and think rather than merely to *feel* in terms fixed finally by Southern patriotism and the prejudices associated with it; men capable of detachment and actively engaged in analysis and criticism of the South itself." [18] Even so, as late as 1940, there were probably fewer than a dozen private and public universities in the South which had fully admitted the modern mind to their campuses and were willing to defend it against public attack. The rest, by avoiding controversial issues, seldom tested the limits of academic freedom, particularly in matters of race and other touchy social and economic relationships of vital interest and importance to the South. Least of all were the politically vulnerable land-grant colleges—whose faculties were closest to the rural heart of these problems—able to investigate them. They stuck very close to their eminently practical and useful knitting of applying physical and natural science to agriculture and letting social science go hang. Their few forays into the neglected social and economic areas amply demonstrated that their normal sense of "the appropriate" was well founded.* Their somewhat better protected sister institutions, the public universities, rarely overstepped the mark either, and even the South's private universities were not often noteworthy for their courage in openly attacking the prevalent social taboos.

During most of the decade following World War II, however, the development of Southern universities, private and public, was truly remarkable. The quality of university faculties was substantially upgraded, in part because regional economic progress was at last reflecting itself in vastly more generous financial support but more important because there was increasing evidence that there was a new freedom for members of Southern faculties to teach, speak, and write on social issues without fear of retaliation or dismissal. In fact, the Southern universities and land-grant colleges finally appeared to be at the threshold of the general renaissance so often hailed in the past but somehow always aborted. Now that the school-integration question has emerged to anger and divide, the fate of Southern higher education once more hangs in the balance.

---

* For example, the dismissal of Dean Carl Taylor, a liberal rural sociologist, of North Carolina State College in 1931; and the attack by Southern Congressmen on the United States Bureau of Agricultural Economics for its unpublished "social survey" of Coahoma County, Miss., in 1945 (Charles M. Hardin, "The Bureau of Agricultural Economics Under Fire: A Study in Valuation Conflicts," *Journal of Farm Economics*, XXVIII [1946], especially 651-55).

Southern Universities and Economic Progress

THOSE who have recently surveyed the Southern temper and state of mind have almost universally warned that the future of the Southern colleges and universities—and as a consequence further regional economic development—is seriously threatened. For example, Ashmore has asserted that despite recent progress in Southern higher education "the region continues to be essentially hostile to the intellectual process—indeed, in the wake of the current racial tension, is perhaps more so than it has been in years. One of the least conspicuous but most significant manifestations of the Negro problem has been its generally stultifying effect upon free inquiry." After quoting Woodward's observation that during the 1830's previously free and open debate on the slavery question gave way before a new test of loyalty to the South, based on conformity of thought and the repression of heresy, Ashmore warned that history may be repeating itself. Today, he said, "The subject of integration in the public schools is off limits for Southern intellectuals; they discuss it only at their peril, and those subject to official reprisal or sensitive to social pressures have been made fully aware of the price they must pay . . . there is no doubt that the great intellectual blight has produced a steady and mounting drain on Southern faculties." [19]

The tragic cost, as Dykeman and Stokely found in their recent survey, may be that some of the colleges and universities of the Deep South will be set back almost beyond repair. They quote a department head at an outstanding Southern university as saying, "In any of our departments here, if you have a vacancy, you can always get somebody from one of the Deep South universities. And nobody will go there . . . [not] even the ones whose homes are there. . . . Any man worth his salt wants to be able to think and

147

speak and work with some degree of inquiry and freedom; he doesn't want to be involved in constant friction and turmoil." [20] If the South's leading private universities and, to a lesser extent, even the Upper South's public institutions have as yet suffered little from this shocking turn of events, it is because their freedom of discussion and right of dissent have thus far been preserved. Even in the Deep South universities, overt offenses against academic freedom and security of tenure have thus far been surprisingly few. But the subtle and informal administrative pressures for discreet silence have sometimes been substantial. With such a stultifying atmosphere, the superior and more independent members of university faculties have been inclined to slip away to better-paying positions elsewhere, leaving vacancies which remain unfilled or are filled with more tractable but less well-qualified successors.

To date, only one Southern college, Alabama Polytechnic Institute (Auburn), has been censured by the American Association of University Professors for violating academic freedom and tenure on race-related grounds. The case involved a decision not to renew the contract of an assistant professor of economics for the sole reason that he had written a letter to the editor of the student newspaper in which he criticized an unfavorable editorial on school integration in New York City. Most of the letter was strictly analytical and even its more emotional and exhortative conclusion was clearly restrained and temperate. However, the Board of Trustees held that the letter was "inflammatory," "irresponsible," and flouted the known opinion of the administration that the institution should be kept free of involvement in the race issue. The Board further asserted that its legal obligations required it to "take such action as it shall deem necessary to protect the institution and its employees from the storms of public controversy which arise from time to time in order that the institution shall be free to discharge its responsibilities in teaching, research, and extension teaching." An editorial in the *Montgomery Advertiser* was more forthright, interpreting this sentence as a rule that "professors must either believe in segregated schools, or keep their mouths shut, or get out."

The AAUP committee which investigated the case phrased it similarly: "If a professor must hold his tongue lest he cause an alumnus to withhold a gift, a legislator to vote against an appropriation, a student not to register, or a citizen's feelings to be ruffled, he will be free to talk only to himself." [21]

Far more significant than such an overt violation of academic freedom, because of its more widespread occurrence in Deep South universities, is the more subtle screening process by which new faculty members are recruited. The Board of the Auburn institution seemed to have no appreciation of the deleterious effects of a screening process on the quality of a faculty. In fact, it offered in partial justification of its decision the claim that the dismissed professor had departed from the explicit understanding under which he had originally been employed. He had, said the Board, been informed at the outset about "the very real tensions surrounding the integration question here in Alabama"; had been advised "that there was no disposition to interfere with his beliefs on that subject"; but had been "warned that if he felt so strongly on the matter as to crusade, or get into controversy, it would be better that he not accept the offer of a position." [22] The dismissed professor denied all this; even if true, this probably common approach in employing members of Deep South universities is bound to outrage (hence eliminate in advance) most of the abler, more sensitive, and more independent applicants.

The probable result is a faculty which is "safe" enough, but only at the expense of analytical ability, social conscience, and personal courage—all desirable attributes in a superior university faculty. Since most of the significant problems of social science must be controversial if they have any current relevance, such a screening process spells death for objective social investigations. Of all university administrators, the most disillusioned are those who believe that by avoiding interpretation (analysis) and "sticking to the facts" Southern social scientists can be productive teachers and research workers without stirring up controversy. If the "facts" are relevant to the current Southern social scene, they are of all things the most controversial to a public which will particularly resent any challenge to its traditional rationalizations of what "everyone knows" the "true" facts are.

Having said so much, however, I should emphasize the relative impotence of any public university before the storms of public emotions and prejudices when aroused. While we should admire those administrators and faculty members who have the courage to resign when the issues clearly warrant it, we should also sympathize with those who, in the same situation, bow to expedience, although it gags them to do so, in order to ride out the storm and restore the authority of reason upon which a university's influence must rest.* What I wish to stress is that in the long run no public university is better than the general public wants it to be. The South's nonacademic intellectual aristocracy faces a tremendous burden of making the general public and its representatives, the university boards of trustees, much more aware that insofar as they deny to their universities the freedom of discussion and dissent they are utterly destroying the very foundations of the institutions which their hard-won tax dollars are so heavily committed to support. Since in the South public feelings on the race question are far more widely held and intense than on the many other issues—pacifism, communism, socialism, and national loyalty †—which have recently brought

* For a very thoughtful analysis of the complexities of the dilemmas of conscience which confront professors and administrators on the present troubled Southern scene, see the article by the chairman of the Department of Philosophy at the University of Alabama, Iredell Jenkins, "Segregation and the Professor," *AAUP Bulletin,* XLIII (1957), 10-18.

† Or oleomargarine, which proved the nemesis of that great land-grant institution, Iowa State College, in 1943! There, the attack came from the state dairy association, incensed by the kind word for oleomargarine which a member of the economics department had to say in a college publication. As one of the seventeen economists who became refugees from that unhappy affair, I am unusually aware of the extent to which outside interference with academic freedom can decimate an eminent faculty even when the general public is far more literate and tolerant than those of most Southern states. Unlike some of the more extreme collegiate situations of the South, however,

American universities into controversy, any hope that the Southern public can be convinced of the necessity of tolerance is expecting a lot. But, if the South is to provide higher education of the quality which further industrial development and its industrially destined youth so desperately need, we can expect no less.

Thus far, I have emphasized the problems of obtaining and preserving excellent faculties in the social sciences. Some Southern university administrators, however, showing the better part of wisdom, have decided to let the social sciences go by the board, preferring to emphasize the less controversial physical and natural sciences whose faculties are also less conscious of and more tractable about their social environment. But this route offers no escape either. Even physicists, soil scientists, and biologists have children; like their social-science colleagues they have an unusually strong passion for having their children well educated; and academic salaries do not easily afford the high tuitions of private schools. The head of the University of Arkansas Medical Center in Little Rock recently stated that because of the school controversy there the Center's "faculty recruitment program [has come] to a virtual standstill." [23] A prominent businessman of Lynchburg, Va., recently warned a committee of the Virginia assembly: "Within the last few weeks the President of one of our colleges has told me of the loss of a good faculty member—a parent of school-age children —who has moved away from Virginia because of the public school situation. Prospective replacements have expressed a disinclination to move into a community where there is a possibility free public schools may not be available for their children." [24]

In a recent state-wide survey of Georgia, James Montgomery, business editor of the *Atlanta Constitution*, polled the administrative, engineering, and research personnel in thirteen major industrial plants and the state's four largest universities. Of the 129 replying,

---

a college president with firmer convictions and a stronger backbone would have been able to fend off the public pressures and prevent the serious academic consequences which actually ensued in Iowa.

one-third said that they intended to leave the state if the public schools were closed for as long as three months to a year. A scientist at the University of Georgia reported that the threat of school closing is "definitely impeding the recruitment of qualified research people for vacancies that remain unfilled in the physical sciences here. So what good will be served by the 12-million-dollar science center we're now building at the university?" [25] Significantly, 60 percent of the students polled at the University of Georgia, and 71 percent of the students at Georgia Tech, preferred desegregation to closing the public schools. Unlike issues of academic freedom, the closing of the public schools is of as direct interest to the faculties of private colleges and universities as it is to those of public institutions. The overwhelming support through petitions by the faculties of Emory University and Agnes Scott College to preserve Georgia's public schools was not only a matter of conviction but a clear-cut effort at self-preservation.[26]

We find that most Southern states, with their eyes firmly fixed on the past, face the problem of keeping their universities as good as they are. Once again North Carolina is demonstrating the sheer commonsense of the alternative of looking to the future both educationally and industrially. Governor Hodges has not only taken a firm stand for the public schools but, building upon his state's excellent universities, has talked local industrialists into financing the establishment of a nonprofit Research Triangle equidistant from the nine hundred scientists of Chapel Hill, Duke University, and North Carolina State College. His foresight in planning for industry's long-run research needs is not only paying off in attracting major new industrial installations to the state but as a by-product offers important new training and employment opportunities for the budding young scientists and engineers of his state. As the proverbial "vale of humility," North Carolina may very well ask in Emerson's words of its immediate and recalcitrant neighboring states, "For what are they all in their high conceit?"

Students of the Southern economy have frequently pointed out that while the migratory flow of the Southern people has been primarily in an outward direction, the flow of college-educated people in the professions and business proprietors and managers has been into the South. Despite its heavy over-all outmigration rates, the South has been able to attract many of the better-educated, better-trained groups upon whose leadership its general educational and economic development so much depends.[27] At the same time, the South's need for importing such groups clearly reflects its shortage of the good universities by which more of its own sons might be enabled to qualify themselves for top positions in Southern industry, education, and the professions. Under present circumstances, this outside talent is essential if Southern universities, and Southern industry, are to rise significantly above their present modest levels of attainment. If we allow our public schools and universities to languish, the vital flow of intellectual capital will be cut off prematurely, seriously impairing both the present economic strength and the further economic progress of the South. Even worse, by preventing the achievement of more adequate Southern education from elementary through graduate school, we will deny to our own youth the opportunity to qualify for the best jobs which our region and nation have to offer.

In higher education as elsewhere, the Southerner has clearly demonstrated the wisdom of Shakespeare's observation that "Praising what is lost makes the remembrance dear." But the danger of this was, as the great bard pointed out elsewhere, that the Southerner,

> ... by telling of it,
> Made such a sinner of his memory,
> To credit his own lie.

In the process, in his state of pathos and self-pity he has resembled those people who, in Douglas Jerrold's words, "are so fond of ill-luck that they run half-way to meet it." In my opinion, it is about time—and probably by now some old Confederate captain would be glad to step into the breach—for a firm command of "About face!"

CHAPTER

7

IF THE SOUTH WANTS ECONOMIC DEVELOPMENT

Brutus. There is a tide in the affairs of men,
Which, taken at the flood, leads on to fortune;
Omitted, all the voyage of their life
Is bound in shallows and in miseries.

— Shakespeare, *Julius Caesar*

A T THE very outset of this book, I stated that the major problem which would concern me here was the following: *if* a majority of Southerners want *as their foremost objective* to achieve higher per capita incomes, what are the barriers to and means of attaining this social end?

But is this in fact what a Southern majority wants? I don't know; but Southern politicians, whose job it is to assess majority opinions, ought to know. Like their constituents, however, most politicians are confused. Certainly there is considerable evidence that Southerners do want more industrialization, which most economists agree is the factor essential to further progress. But few Southerners have yet faced up to the question of whether they want industrialization badly enough to give up firmly held Southern traditions which are inconsistent with it. And fewer politicians yet have had the fore-sight or the courage to make clear to their constituents that a funda-mental choice between Southern economic development and cher-ished traditions must be made.

Senator Fulbright of Arkansas recently extolled the goal of re-gional economic development in the following words: "The South is no longer the nation's No. 1 economic problem; it is now the na-tion's new economic frontier. The level of economic development in the South is still considerably below that of the rest of the nation. However, we no longer view our difficulties as a national problem, but as a challenge to ourselves; a challenge to develop our potentials to reach the national level of economic development so that the people of the South may share fully in the American standard of living." [1] Yet Senator Fulbright has had to tread very lightly on the matters of tradition raised by the school-integration issue in his state, where he faces the fact of Representative Brooks Hays's de-feat and the threat of Governor Faubus as a potential rival for his Senate seat. On the other hand, the full costs to Arkansas of the Faubus fiasco have gradually come to light.

Therefore, if most Southern states today stand at the crossroads between tradition and progress, their choice may be the wiser be-cause of the increasingly strong evidence that Arkansas took the wrong turn. Although the atmosphere is still murky, it appears that in Tennessee and North Carolina, and probably in Florida and Virginia as well, moderate political leadership has now recognized the necessity of choosing between tradition and progress and has firmly chosen progress. On the other hand, most political leaders in the Deep South appear to have chosen tradition—a choice epito-mized by the vow of Governor Vandiver of Georgia that "There will be no mixing in the class rooms come hell or high water"—al-though they may still be under the false illusion that tradition and progress are not irreconcilable. That the two goals are in fact ir-reconcilable was well expressed by Ralph McGill when he wrote that Southern leaders "seeking new enterprises never saw them-selves as carriers of the virus which was to destroy the *status quo* in their towns . . .—and also, therefore, the old 'way of life in the South.' . . . They sought with a kind of desperation to maintain the *status quo*—all the while laboring to bring new industries and pay-rolls which could only accelerate the changes." [2]

Thus, the South has been choosing progress over tradition almost in spite of itself and has done it so gradually as to be largely unaware of what was happening. However, progress by drift is at best bound to be slow enough, and unless the South faces the conflicts between tradition and progress squarely and realistically, its stubborn and recently intensified adherence to tradition may well slow progress to a snail's pace at the very time when its rapid acceleration might normally have been expected. In this final chapter, therefore, I shall first summarize those aspects of Southern tradition which I have already argued at length do seriously impede economic progress. I shall then present a positive program of economic policies which would significantly facilitate further regional progress, followed by a closing word which takes a cautiously optimistic view of the South's economic future.

Tradition as a Barrier to Progress: A Summary

IN ITS recent advertisements, The Southern Company has declared: "The march has just begun! The last half of the twentieth century belongs to the South!" Whether or not such extravagant claims are possible of fulfilment is still unsettled. To the extent that the South still belongs to the nineteenth century, it must fail to make its full and wholly realizable claim to the twentieth. Let me attempt to summarize briefly here my previous analysis of those elements in the Southern tradition which have seriously impeded its economic progress.

In Chapter 2, I noted the effects of the dominant agrarian values in the Southern heritage. Early American tradition combined the philosophy of agrarianism with a strong spirit of progress. The South embraced agrarianism but, with its burgeoning system of slavery and plantation, lost interest in progress even with reference to agriculture. Increasingly, in ante-bellum days the South's dominant agrarianism took the form of a positive antagonism toward industrial-urban development as an inferior way of life. With defeat and Reconstruction, the South's agrarian philosophy first came into serious question, but the region's frenzied efforts to industrialize produced only modest results, so that the traditional agrarian values were ultimately reinforced and largely restored to a position of dominance. As a consequence, agrarianism impeded balanced and broadly based regional economic progress in the following ways: (1) It created an agrarian-oriented scale of social prestige, which has directed a disproportionate share of the South's indigenous capital into agricultural rather than business assets and too much of its superior human talent into nonbusiness fields. (2) It insulated the large planter from competing economic forces, which otherwise might have weakened his excessive social, political, and economic hold upon his local community. (3) It perpetuated a strong love of the land and outdoor life, which has discouraged human mobility and created a belief that Southerners are unsuited for the discipline of the factory system. (4) It made a tradition of leisure, which has discouraged economic enterprise on the part of the wealthy class and has produced, and even given sanction to, laziness and lassitude on the part of poor whites and Negroes.

In Chapter 3, I considered at length the effects of the South's rigid social structure. The Revolution largely ended the tendency in America to take over the British system of large landholdings and a socio-politically dominant landed aristocracy. However, the British pattern, already firmly established in the Southern Tidewater in colonial days, became the model for a new planter aristocracy which waxed fat on the rich new combination of cotton, slavery, and plantation after 1800. The consequence was an environment unusually favorable to the perpetuation of a carefully stratified rural society in which first the Negro, and later the typical white, had his place. Whereas the rest of the United States largely rejected the aristocratic ideal derived from England, the South took it over as a major element in its value system. As in England, the new Southern aristocracy at its best accepted *noblesse oblige*, which made the social system sufficiently attractive to win rather general acceptance by the masses of yeoman farmers and poor whites.

The net effects of this rural social structure on regional economic progress were distinctly unfavorable for the following reasons: (1) The aristocratic ideal was seriously corrupted through its association with the positive defense of slavery before the Civil War and with white supremacy after the war. (2) The spirit of extreme individualism became increasingly dominant over *noblesse oblige*, so that the aristocrat increasingly held that his less fortunate neighbors were wholly responsible for themselves rather than being either his responsibility or a product of the social system. (3) There was an abnormal subordination of the Southern rural middle class, which was unable to contribute nearly as much to the democratization and economic development of its region as did its counterpart in the other American regions. (4) The South took on a backward-looking, pessimistic, and static outlook which was the natural product of its status society as the region emerged from the ordeal of military defeat. (5) The South's upper classes came to accept as normal and inevitable socio-economic arrangements based on a disproportionate number of low-income people, arrangements made tolerable to lower-income rural whites by a social structure which at least clearly supported their claims to superiority over the Negro race. (6) The relatively rigid, rural social substructure gave little ground to the development of Southern cities which, despite their more fluid social substructures and their growing urban middle classes, were handicapped by inadequate growth rates and a discriminatory political structure.

In Chapter 4, I emphasized the effects of the South's undemocratic political structure. We saw there how early interregional conflicts of economic interests over the tariff and slavery formed the political basis for the South's sectionalism and ultimately for the Civil War. During this period a relatively small minority of large slaveholders not only were able to persuade most of their white neighbors to take up arms in defense of slavery but also succeeded in defeating the threat of post-bellum agrarian radicalism by raising the battle-cry of white supremacy. The consequence was a monolithic political structure, based on the overriding end of maintaining white supremacy whatever the cost, which has seriously impeded regional economic progress in the following ways: (1) It embodied a blind sectionalism which has encouraged the trend toward coercive federalism instead of toward a healthy federalism under which the nation's resources might be used to promote greater regional balance in economic development. (2) It embraced a negative and defensive States' Rights doctrine which, too narrowly based on considerations of race, has offered a serious political impediment to much-needed federal grants-in-aid to the low-income South. (3) It was based upon a narrow electorate, reflecting not only restrictions on the suffrage of most Negroes and many whites but also low voter-participation rates attributable to a one-party system and the generally low educational and income status of much of the citizenry. (4) Consequently, it gave a disproportionate political influence to Black Belt whites relative to Negroes and low-income rural whites. (5) It insulated rural political leaders from the political counterforces of Southern industrial-urban development, because of the general failure of legislatures to reapportion legislative districts in response to radical rural-urban population shifts. (6) It perpetuated political control by a coalition of economic conservatives and racial extremists who continue to use racial antagonism as a means of maintaining the status quo against the liberalizing influences of the new social forces abroad in the South.

In Chapter 5, I examined the effects of the weakness of social responsibility in the Southern tradition, particularly as reflected in inadequate support for public-school education. Even before the Civil War, the development of public-school systems in the South was severely handicapped by the preference of the dominant planter class for private schools and the general view that public schools were "schools for paupers." Although Reconstruction brought a partial social revolution which for the first time established a sound basis for the public financing of common-school systems in the South, the indifference or even antagonism of the dominant socio-economic class seriously inhibited the general advancement of public education. At the same time, the dominant class has allowed its self-interest in perpetuating a cheap labor supply to override any feeling of general social responsibility for the economic development of the local community.

This weakness of social responsibility on the part of the South's traditional socio-political leadership has been a formidable barrier to regional economic progress in several ways: (1) It has kept the masses of Southern people, white and Negro, in relative ignorance in a world in which knowledge and skills are increasingly the key to both personal and social betterment. (2) It has led responsible political leaders to propose abolition of public schools as a solution to the school-integration controversy, without regard for the educational needs of the vast majority of their people or for the effects on concurrent industrialization campaigns. (3) It has caused large planters and the managers of local low-wage industries to oppose measures to facilitate outmigration and local industrialization, despite the general community interest in such developments. (4) It has encouraged a continued belief that the South's low-income people are poor because they are innately inferior, rationalizing a policy of inaction toward the improvement of schools and other public services and the attainment of a more efficient and equitable social and economic organization. (5) It has resulted in a too-easy approval of the recent high outmigration rates by Southern Negroes, which, while undoubtedly contributing to an easing of racial tensions, must increasingly represent a substantial social loss—in terms of potential industrial labor force and prior public educational investments—to the states from which they migrate.

Finally, in Chapter 6, I discussed the intellectually debilitating effects of the Southern tradition of conformity of thought and behavior. The South's extreme cultural and ethnic homogeneity was transformed into strait-jacket conformity and intolerance of dissent, first by intersectional rivalry before the Civil War and later by solidification against the vindictive forces of the Reconstruction period. In rejecting Yankee thought and the Yankee mind, Southerners closed their minds on every other important social doctrine as well. The results were a general intolerance of intellectualism, an acceptance of violence as an ultimate weapon against nonconformity and dissent, and a corruption of higher education as it too increasingly repudiated innovation and novelty in thought and behavior. In all these respects, the Southern tradition of conformity has been a serious handicap to regional economic progress. (1) It created an environment hostile to the use of intellectual processes as a means to technological and social innovation and advancement, with consequent intellectual stagnation and the draining off of the South's best intellectual and industrial talent into other regions. (2) It gave public acceptance of, and often official sanction to, the use of violence as a means of enforcing conformity, even though an atmosphere of law and order is a fundamental condition for attracting industrial plants from other regions. (3) It seriously threatened both the academic freedom and the public-school base which are so vital to the development of great Southern universities and without which the South cannot attract and hold superior faculties, develop its own indigenous industrial and intellectual leaders, or provide the research and training facilities which are a prerequisite for sound and broadly based industrialization of the South.

In this book, I have asserted that the South must choose between tradition and progress. It must choose because, as the above summation makes abundantly clear, Southern tradition has essential elements—its value system, social and political structure, weakness of social responsibility, intolerance of nonconformity and the intellectual process *—which are irreconcilably at war with regional economic progress. If Southerners generally choose progress (as I do), how may they best throw off the heavy burden of the past and get on with the task at hand?

* In my initial prospectus of this book, I also intended to include as another element in the Southern tradition its "other-worldly religion." However, upon further reflection, I decided to omit this important matter. Even so, I should perhaps make explicit the extent to which, quite apart from the lessons of social science, my own maturing interpretation and application of Christian teachings have influenced my attitudes toward race relations. I have been forced to conclude that, quite apart from their economic and social aspects, traditional Southern racial attitudes inescapably have a moral aspect as well. That so few of my co-religionists in the South seem to see this moral issue never ceases to discourage and amaze me. It is a paradox that the South, which by every objective standard is the most religious region in America, could be so blind to the practical implications of Christianity. Somehow the Southern religious tradition has never progressed from the Old Testament's God of Wrath to the New Testament's God of Love and Brotherhood, nor from an ethereal concern for the other world to a concrete moral concern for social injustice in the here and now. In my view, Southern religious attitudes have been hopelessly schizophrenic and outrageously self-righteous.

On the race issue, it is the South's moral leadership which has been found most wanting, particularly in terms of what might be most reasonable to expect. For every Brooks Hays, there have been a hundred lay leaders of the Southern church who have remained silent or worse. For every minister of the Gospel who has, individually or collectively, spoken out, there have been scores who have followed rather than led their flocks. To me, the importance of religion has been one of the finest elements in the Southern tradition. But if we are not to make a mockery of this grand religious heritage, can we Southerners any longer refuse to carry it to its logical and spiritual conclusion?

A Positive Program for Southern Economic Progress

In the last section of Chapter 1, I emphasized that the South's poverty problem is centered in its nonfarm Negro population and in its farm families, both white and Negro. Of these two low-income groups, the former probably faces less serious economic straits than the latter. Rural-urban income comparisons are inherently difficult because of the problems of measuring the greater income in kind (housing and home-produced food) which farmers enjoy. The available income statistics do support the view that most Negro families of the urban South have higher real incomes than do the South's Negro farm families and that they are in fact better off than substantial numbers of the South's white farm families. Furthermore, even though the wide income differentials between urban whites and urban Negroes in the South reflect the effects of race discrimination as well as differences in education, job training, and the like, an urban environment does offer the Southern Negro a better opportunity to overcome the latter "real" disadvantages so that, as the force of race discrimination becomes weaker, he can more easily close the prevailing interracial income gap. In low-income rural areas, on the other hand, both whites and Negroes face economic disadvantages, largely unrelated to race, which account for a major part of the poverty of both groups and in the process keep racial antagonisms very much alive. While I shall return to the race problem as such in the next section, I want to center attention in this section upon those economic policies by which the South's rural poverty may be alleviated to the benefit of both races.

For reasons already indicated late in Chapter 1, I believe that a solution to the problem of the South's low-income rural areas requires an acceleration of the rate of industrial-urban development throughout the region.

If the South Wants Economic Development

What public policies would facilitate industrial-urban development?

First, the Southern legislatures need to give much greater financial support to their state industrial development commissions, which particularly need to strengthen their research and planning programs, both technical and economic. Far too much of the Southern states' limited industrial promotion funds are being spent on such general and largely irrelevant claims as the 99 percent Anglo-Saxon composition of the (white!) labor force, the excellence of the natural climate, and the docility and cheapness of the Southern worker. The hard-headed industrialist deciding where to locate a plant is interested in such objective information as the amount and chemical analysis of the available water resources, the subsoil conditions of alternative plant sites, the structure of freight rates, the extent of local public services, and the efficiency of local government. An effective industrial development commission must have a staff of competent chemists, geologists, engineers, economists, and public administrators who can supply industrialists with the accurate information they need and who can help local governments to develop more adequate public services on the most efficient basis possible. At the same time, Southern governors and other public officials must support these promotional campaigns by maintaining law and order and strengthening the public-school systems rather than undermine them by permitting violence and closing the schools.

Second, federal public-power policy must recognize the need for an adequate expansion of the supply of electric power to take care of the Tennessee Valley's future industrial needs. In the heat of the debate over public versus private power, the proponents of TVA have gone overboard in their defense of public power and cheap power rates. They have lost sight of the fundamental issue, which is an adequate power supply, whether public or private. With government installations at Oak Ridge, Paducah, and Tullahoma taking over half of TVA's power output, TVA has increasingly become a subsidiary power plant of the federal government to the detriment of private industrial expansion. Furthermore, cheap rates are of no avail if the supply of TVA power is insufficient to meet the industrial demand at these low rates—in part because of inadequate expansion of power-producing facilities, but also in part because TVA's present rate structure encourages waste and uneconomic uses (such as home heating) of power in households when this same power might contribute more to regional economic progress if it were diverted to industrial uses instead. If the Tennessee Valley is not to be at a serious disadvantage in relation to other Southern regions which are served by rapidly expanding private utilities, Congress must either give TVA sufficient autonomy to permit it to keep pace with its area's industrial needs or abolish it altogether. The middle course—by which Congress simply hamstrings TVA because it represents public power—offers the greatest danger to progress, since, as long as public competition prevails in the valley, private utilities will certainly not be willing to make up the existing serious deficiency in the valley's power supply. The TVA Act of 1959, granting the Authority substantial new powers of self-financing, may well have largely solved this problem. But the matter is important enough to deserve close watching.

Third, federal labor-market information and employment statistics need to be redesigned to recognize the widespread condition of agricultural underemployment throughout the Southern region. According to our national employment statistics, virtually all people gainfully employed in agriculture are tacitly considered fully employed, although many of them are part-time seasonal workers at best. The United States Department of Labor's monthly reports on "labor-surplus" market areas are limited to urban centers with substantial industrial unemployment. Such reports need to be extended to include rural areas with large surpluses of underemployed farm labor, in order to bring out into the open the considerable amount of hidden unemployment even under statistical full-employment conditions. If this were done, more industrialists might be attracted to such rural areas. At the same time, Congress might well specify that in the interest of dispersing prime industrial military targets the federal government should, other things being equal, favor location in such rural areas through its financing of new defense plants and the letting of defense contracts.

Fourth, there is a serious need for much more generous public support for the improvement of Southern educational and health facilities. I shall consider this matter more fully in connection with policies for facilitating labor mobility, but its importance to the promotion of Southern industrialization warrants at least its mention at this point as well.

These and other measures to speed the rate of economically sound industrialization in the rural South should have a very high priority as the South attacks its low-income farm problem. However, a word of caution is essential at this point. It is not likely that the rate of industrialization in the South can possibly be great enough over the next generation to solve by itself the low-income problem. Without migration, the South's low-income farming areas must currently find local nonfarm employment for one out of every two farm males entering the productive age-group of twenty to sixty-four even to maintain present conditions.[3] They must find far more nonfarm employment, either locally or at a distance, if the ratio of population to agricultural resources is to be significantly improved.

It is therefore obvious that while we should try to minimize the need for human outmigration by encouraging industrial development of low-income areas, a substantial rate of outmigration from most low-income rural counties will continue to be a necessity. This is particularly true of those counties which lack many of the prerequisites necessary to attract any but the least desirable types of industrial plants. Because of the economic requirements of large-scale production and of location, we certainly cannot expect a General Motors plant in every county seat. Perhaps the most we can hope for is that most low-income rural areas will find it possible to attract at least some industries which will upgrade local employment and payrolls to a limited extent; and that a limited number of urban and metropolitan centers within each state can industrialize sufficiently more rapidly to hold much of the population within the state if not within the local community.

If this view is correct, it means that the people of particular low-income rural counties cannot study their problem effectively independent of their interrelationships with the urban centers of the broader economic areas of which they are a part. It also means that however much low-income rural counties may deplore the loss of population by outmigration, they cannot afford to limit their efforts to the attraction of local industry. Instead, the welfare of their future farm population still necessitates simultaneous and equally vigorous attention to facilitating outmigration of their surplus farm people and inmigration of additional farm capital. Certainly they should prefer having substantially fewer local farm families with relatively high farm incomes to having three or four times as many families with wholly inadequate farm incomes. Thus, the most effective efforts to industrialize low-income rural areas must still be accompanied by more adequate attention to promoting the mobility of both farm people and farm capital.

What public policies will facilitate the outmigration of surplus farm population?

First and most important, we must have federal monetary and fiscal policies which will maintain a stable and expanding national economy. As long as we continue to have general prosperity and industrial expansion, the South should benefit most, because it has the major pool of under-utilized labor for manning the nation's new manufacturing plants and service industries. At the same time, even a mild business recession quickly dams up the normal outward flow of Southern people, to the detriment of both region and nation.

Second, Congress must recognize that even under conditions of national prosperity, private industrial price and wage policies offer serious barriers to the ready access of underemployed rural people to nonfarm labor markets. If industrial monopolies restrict the expansion of output and employment and if strong labor unions restrict the entry of new workers, the combined effect is likely to be underemployment in nonfarm labor markets as well. In other words, whether fixed by collective bargaining or by minimum wage laws, prevailing wage rates may become so high that they attract a supply of industrial labor greater than the demand for such labor, forcing the rationing of jobs by arbitrary hiring practices and union rules. Such a result works strongly to the disadvantage of the low-income worker who would like to shift from farm to nonfarm employment. Congress needs therefore to develop a national employment policy in which more rigorous enforcement of the anti-trust laws and the revision of restrictive union practices and labor legislation would probably play a major role.

Third, all levels of government must give much more adequate financial support for education and health facilities. Industrial demands for labor are increasingly selective in favor of higher levels of education and skills. The people of the South's low-income rural areas are seriously disadvantaged in competing for industrial jobs on such a basis because of the major deficiencies in their public-school systems and their medical, health, and library facilities. Furthermore, the South's rural youths have virtually no access to vocational training and counselling services except the traditional vocational agriculture programs which assume that they will be farmers when the vast majority clearly will not be. Most Southern state and local governments could undoubtedly support general education, nonfarm vocational training, and library and public health facilities more adequately than they do if more community leaders assumed the full burden of social responsibility which they have so long neglected. Even if Southern community leadership were more generally public-spirited, these vital public services will continue to fall substantially short of desirable levels unless the South's financial resources are supplemented by generous federal grants-in-aid.

In my opinion, the case in favor of federal aid to education and related services is very strong. The South has chronically faced the dilemma of having much lower per capita incomes and a much larger proportion of young people than do other regions. As a result, although it devotes larger relative shares of its state and local budgets to education, the South cannot afford nearly as high absolute levels of school expenditures per school child as can the richer states in other parts of the nation. At the same time, because of its higher birth rates and its shortage of nonfarm job opportunities, the South must on balance "export" a major part of its youth to the richer states. After having invested its very scarce private and public resources in rearing and educating its children, the South loses millions of them as soon as they reach their productive years. (A recent University of Tennessee study estimated that this drain on the investment in youth through outmigration amounts to about $135,-000,000 annually for Tennessee alone.) The South fails to reap any return on much of its hard-won investment in its young people, while the richer states reap a substantial return and bear little or none of these preparation costs. Even so, many Southern migrants have far less education and training than the richer host states would probably prefer. Only through federal aid can the richer regions help to support Southern education, thereby equalizing the fiscal burden among the several regions.

Curiously enough, among the principal opponents of federal aid to education are the South's Congressional delegations. Their position undoubtedly reflects to some extent the traditional dim view of public education which has been so characteristic of much of the South's socio-political leadership. Some attack federal aid on the grounds that the states, after sending their tax money to Washington, receive substantially less back because of the federal government's "handling costs." Such logic would be unassailable if per capita incomes were nearly equal in all fifty states, but with the great inequalities which actually prevail it ignores the fact that the poor Southern states would in any case receive much more in educational benefits than they pay out in federal taxes. The most important argument is that federal aid means federal control—an argument which in general terms falls on its face in the light of nearly a century of federally supported land-grant colleges whose independence and autonomy have been scrupulously preserved. So far as the Southern opposition to federal aid of public-school education is concerned, "federal controls" is a euphemism for "federally en-forced school integration." But it should be clear by now that the South must inevitably face this particular "federal control," with or without federal aid. One hopes that Southern whites will at last learn the fruitlessness of perversely allowing the race problem to force them once more to cut off their noses to spite their faces.

Fourth, the United States Employment Service should receive much greater financial support so that it can increase considerably its number of offices in low-income rural counties where job infor-mation services are most needed. Given its present spotty geo-graphic coverage and inadequate field staff, the federal-state depart-ment of employment security can service the more rural counties only a few days each month. Most of its energies are of necessity directed toward the processing of unemployment compensation claims rather than toward supplying adequate job information. This agency particularly needs to find means of helping unskilled work-ers find employment elsewhere and to develop for particular low-income communities new channels of migration to industrial cities other than those to which these communities are already tied through past migration of relatives and friends.

Fifth, in cooperation with the local offices of the employment service, urban welfare agencies, both public and private, need to develop a more positive and better coordinated program to assist migrants from low-income rural areas in making the difficult eco-nomic, social, and psychological adjustments associated with a radi-cally new way of life. With few exceptions (notably Cincinnati), Northern and Western cities have seriously neglected this poignant human problem.

What public policies can facilitate the movement of additional farm capital (and concomitant managerial assistance) into low-income rural areas?

The farm capital problem is perhaps the most difficult aspect of the broader problem of low-income rural areas because, with oc-casional exceptions, additional farm capital cannot be effectively used within present farm boundaries. In general, the boundaries of individual farms (remaining family owned and operated) must be considerably expanded and the supply of skilled farm managers increased before the development of livestock enterprises and of mechanization becomes economically sound. In other words, in most low-income rural areas agriculture must ultimately be reorganized into substantially fewer family farms on a community-wide basis—a reorganization which must await a substantial reduction in the pressure of farm population on local land resources and a consequent reduction in land values. Hence the farm capital problem of necessity must be divided into its short- and long-run aspects.

In a short-run context, the principal farm capital needs of low-income rural areas are several. First, commercial banks, the agencies of the Farm Credit Administration, and the Farmers Home Administration need to develop a coordinated farm credit policy, with particular attention to meeting intermediate-term credit needs and expanding the managerial services which accompany the extension of credit to individual farmers. Second, within the broader framework, prompt attention should be given to meeting fully the credit and managerial needs of those individual low-income farmers who show the greatest initiative and promise in reorganizing their farming operations on a larger scale and a more efficient basis. The improvement of such pilot farms will require both careful planning and detailed supervision by agricultural experiment stations, agricultural extension workers, and the field staffs of credit agencies.

Third, credit facilities for helping small farmers to develop intensive farm enterprises (such as broilers, eggs, or strawberries) which will increase their incomes without enlargement of the landholdings should also receive attention. (Here, as the development of the Southern broiler industry has demonstrated, private middlemen may make a substantial contribution through credit and managerial assistance to small farmers.) There will be, however, a strong temptation to press new intensive enterprises much too far because they require fewer population adjustments and little land consolidation. This temptation should be resisted since in the absence of particularly favorable locations near major urban centers, such enterprises will frequently fall short of assuring satisfactory net farm incomes, particularly if generalized to the point where expanding supplies cause substantial price declines.

Within a long-run context, the principal farm capital needs of low-income rural areas may best be met as follows. First, agricultural research, extension, and credit personnel need to pool their resources in working out on a pilot basis some community-wide plans of the adjustments in human, land, and capital resources required to attain the goal of a high-productivity, high-income agriculture. Such plans should seek to establish community goals, indicating how much local farm population must be reduced by local industry or outmigration and how much supervised farm credit needs to be expanded to achieve long-run agricultural reorganization of the given low-income community. (Such a long-run community plan would also be useful as a guide in assuring that short-run farm credit policy in the local community will be consistent with desirable long-run agricultural development.)

Second, Congress should substantially increase the lending authority and supervisory personnel of the Farmers Home Administration, the federal agency created specifically to ameliorate the farm credit needs of the low-income farmer. Thus far, the resources of the Farmers Home Administration have been so small that they have been spread too thinly to contribute significantly to the drastic community-wide reorganization of agriculture which a solution of the low-income farm problem requires. Instead, an experimental program of local saturation lending should be initiated, with much larger amounts of supervised credit per farm permitted where heavy past outmigration and other conditions are favorable for community-wide readjustments in farm boundaries and crop-livestock combinations. The farm capital needs of low-income rural areas are so vast that small loans may do more harm than good. Bold experimentation with carefully supervised loans for much larger amounts than those normally considered prudent, while initially foolhardy as a matter of general policy, would appear to be fully warranted on a pilot basis. Where such large loans prove to be a mistake, they should be written off as a cost of experimentation, but if the general experience is largely favorable, general public farm credit policy should be revised accordingly.

Let me close this section by summarizing briefly my analysis of the South's vast problem of low-income rural areas. In Chapter 1, I indicated that far more families are trying to make a living from farming than Southern agricultural resources can possibly support at a level of living comparable with that afforded by similar non-farm occupations. Rural poverty in the South is community-wide and, because it has deep historical and cultural roots, tends to be self-perpetuating. A high rate of outmigration from the South's low-income rural areas is essential but, as history has already proved, cannot by itself solve the problem of rural poverty. Insofar as practicable, industrialization of the South's rural areas is highly desirable but is unlikely to proceed at a rate sufficient to warrant neglect of policies to facilitate outmigration and to increase the availability of farm credit. There is no single, simple solution to the problem of low-income rural areas. Above all, as I emphasized in Chapter 2, agricultural price supports and the soil bank cannot help appreciably the low-income problem of farmers who produce little and work little land. Yet such programs, because of their great cost, strongly divert public funds and public concern from a million or more farm families who require substantial and sustained public assistance.

In the present chapter, I have tried to show that if we are to solve the problem of the South's community-wide rural poverty during the next generation we must devise a coordinated, integrated, and well-financed set of public policies which will at the same time encourage industrial development, facilitate outmigration, and expand supervised farm credit in low-income rural areas. Anything short of such a three-pronged attack on rural poverty (with general, nonfarm vocational, and farm-management education playing a major role on all three fronts) will almost surely be wholly insufficient and inadequate.

But what of the Rural Development Program, now nearly four years old, of the United States Department of Agriculture? The present administration deserves strong praise for initiating this new program, which is specifically aimed at helping to solve the primarily Southern low-income rural problem. Unfortunately, this problem is far too vast and deep-seated to be solved by the Rural Development Program as presently conceived. While the cautious grass-roots approach of this program may have been largely justifiable up to date, it will have to become much more sharply focused, better integrated and coordinated, much bolder in its objectives, and far better financed if it is to make significant inroads in reducing the South's widespread rural poverty. This program has placed its emphasis too exclusively upon only one essential ingredient of progress—local initiative and enterprise. The other essential ingredient—outside financial and technical assistance, both public and private—has been largely ignored and neglected. Such a onesided approach seriously obscures the basic fact that, with their own very limited resources, the South's low-income rural communities cannot solve their problems with the best of local leadership and cooperation; and it reinforces the unfortunate cultural heritage and narrow socio-political outlook of many state and local leaders, thereby tending to preserve rather than to change the status quo in low-income rural areas.

The leaders of the Rural Development Program have effectively identified the principal elements of the low-income rural problem and many of the public policies appropriate to its solution. However, they have failed to recognize the full magnitude of the governmental assistance required, particularly on the financial and managerial side, for achieving an ultimate resolution of the problem. If my analysis in this chapter is correct, the greatest remaining needs are large increases in federal appropriations and grants-in-aid for improved general and vocational education, for a much greater amount of supervised farm credit, for more special agricultural research and extension services, for more adequate labor market information and employment services, and for better health facilities in rural areas. Costly though such programs would be, they could be easily financed by diversion to this purpose of a relatively small part of the amounts now expended on farm price-support programs. In view of the present stupendous waste of human resources in the South's low-income rural areas, can we afford to do any less?

Wanted: Emancipation of the Southern White

IF ANY single generalization emerges from our analysis of Southern tradition, viewed from whatever angle, it is that the race issue dominates all other elements of the picture. While the Negro was physically emancipated from the Southern white in 1862, the psychological emancipation of the Southern white from the Negro is yet to be achieved a century later. As Jonathan Daniels recently put it, "The whites have sometimes seemed to carry segregation to the point of insisting upon carrying the Negro as a load." [4] Yet, as a low-income region the South is peculiarly ill-equipped to carry this self-imposed load, which has so heavily drained off the region's energies from the constructive channels leading to economic progress. I do not believe that Key has exaggerated in concluding his *Southern Politics* with the following words: "until greater emancipation of the white from the Negro is achieved, the southern political and economic system will labor under formidable handicaps. The race issue broadly defined thus must be considered as the number one problem on the southern agenda. Lacking a solution for it, all else fails." [5]

While one might easily despair about finding such a solution in the present disturbed Southern scene, I believe that it can and will be done. As solid as the race-oriented traditions of the South appear to be, they are being steadily weakened by the much more solid economic progress that the South has already made and, with patient and wise leadership, will continue to make. Let us therefore look for a moment at the extent of the South's general economic development since 1930.

During the last three decades, the South has enjoyed a substantial rate of industrialization.[6] Between 1929 and 1947 alone, for example, the South's share of the nation's total value added by manufacture increased from 10 to 14 percent and has undoubtedly tended to gain on the rest of the nation since that time. During 1929-47 the South's per capita value added by manufacture increased from 37 to 53 percent of the national average * and from 30 to 45 percent of the average for the non-South. By 1950, the 11 percent of the Southern work force engaged in the manufacturing of non-durable goods was nearly equal to that (12 percent) of the non-South's work force similarly engaged. However, in typically higher-productivity, higher-wage durable goods manufacturing, relative employment in the South (7 percent) still lagged far behind that in the non-South (17 percent). Thus, in 1950, only 18 percent of Southern workers were employed in *all* manufacturing as compared with 29 percent of the workers outside the South. However, these data indicate that while the interregional gap in industrial development remains large, it has been closing at a heartening rate.

With the South's continuing industrial development since 1930, its urbanization has proceeded apace. During 1930-50, the South's urban population increased from 34 to 44 percent and since 1950 it has undoubtedly passed the 50 percent level, with the South thereby becoming more urban than rural some fifty years later than the rest of the nation. Despite urbanization, however, the Southern population's rate of natural increase increased in absolute terms during 1940-50, although not nearly so much as that of the population

---

* For the longer period 1929-54, selected states showed the following gains in per capita value added (United States average=100): South Carolina 37 to 62 percent, Georgia 41 to 58 percent, Tennessee 48 to 69 percent, Virginia 60 to 64 percent, Ohio constant at 174 percent, and Iowa 50 to 64 percent. (Cf., pp. 27-28.)

of the non-South. As a result, while the historical interregional differential in fertility rates—twice as high in the South as in the non-South as late as 1940—largely disappeared in the interim, it was not because the South's rate of population growth declined but because of the "baby boom" in other regions. Thus, the South's substantial industrial development was by no means sufficient fully to relieve the economic pressures which favored large-scale outmigration. As a result, eleven Southern states lost by net outmigration during 1930-50 some 3,800,000 people (44 percent Negro), while five other peripheral Southern states and the District of Columbia were gaining nearly 1,600,000 inmigrants (only 5 percent Negro). If these two groups are combined into a single "Census South," we find that some 2,200,000 people (72 percent Negro) migrated to destinations even beyond the greater South.* This preponderance of Negro migrants reflects the greater difficulties they face in finding nonfarm employment in the Southern region. As a consequence, the South's relative Negro population (which had been 34 percent in 1900) declined from 26 to 22 percent during 1930-50.

Under the combined influences of Southern industrialization and outmigration, the South's relative rural population declined from 66 to 54 percent during 1930-50. The decline in the relative importance of agricultural employment was much greater, from 43 to only 23 percent. As a result of the diminished pressure of the rural population on the South's limited agricultural resources, the average size of farms increased significantly and farm tenancy dropped substantially during 1930-50,† thereby at last reversing

* Compiled or computed from Lee *et al.*, *Population Redistribution and Economic Growth*. In this compilation, the first group of states includes West Virginia, North Carolina, South Carolina, Georgia, Kentucky, Tennessee, Alabama, Mississippi, Arkansas, Louisiana, and Oklahoma, all of which had persistent outmigration during 1930-50; the second group includes Florida, Texas, Delaware, the District of Columbia, and (reflecting in part the suburban growth of the District of Columbia) Virginia and Maryland, all of which had net immigration.

† For selected states, the average number of acres of land per farm increased as follows: South Carolina 66 to 85, Georgia 86 to 130, Tennessee

unfavorable trends of half a century or more. Nonetheless, as late as 1949, the average Southern farm and farm worker lagged far behind the national average in resources, productivity, and income. Even in the South's potentially richest agricultural area, the Mississippi Delta, the average farm—which used almost as much labor but 58 percent less cropland and 68 percent less capital than the nation's average farm—had a net value of output per worker which was only 62 percent of the national average. Less well-endowed agricultural areas of the South, of course, made an even poorer showing. As I pointed out earlier, the South's average farm family had a net cash income from all sources which was just over one-half of its counterpart in the non-South. For such reasons, it is obvious that as great as the South's recent rates of industrialization and outmigration have been, the rather drastic program of public policies which I outlined earlier in this chapter is still needed by the South's many remaining low-income rural people.

It is easy to lose one's perspective in such a matter. The fact remains that, as our best over-all indicator shows, per capita incomes in the South did increase from 47 to 64 percent of the non-South's during 1929-48 and have fluctuated at around 68 percent in more recent years. If there is any ground for discouragement, it lies in the fact that the South's per capita income made relatively little further gain on the rest of the nation during 1948-54 and that more recently

---

73 to 80, and Virginia 98 to 103. The corresponding reductions in the percentage of farms operated by tenants were: South Carolina 65 to 45, Georgia 68 to 43, Tennessee 46 to 29, and Virginia 28 to 17. These data make clear that states whose agriculture is more generally organized on a plantation basis (indirectly indicated by relatively higher tenancy rates) found it easier to increase average farm size. The reason is that with a number of sharecropping land units (each a census "farm") already under common ownership, the planter can easily reassign his relatively large and contiguous landholdings to fewer tenants, thereby increasing the acreage in each remaining operating unit (farm). In states where small owner-operated landholdings are more typical, however, the barriers to land consolidation by purchase are much more formidable.

the intensification of race conflict has raised a serious threat to still further regional economic progress. Since so much of the South's traditional race antagonism has had its roots in community-wide rural poverty, one major contribution to its solution clearly lies in the additional industrial-urban development by which such poverty can be largely eliminated.

With Southern urbanization, more and more Negroes (and poor whites) are able to escape to an environment which, despite all of its limitations, offers far less formidable obstacles to political participation and economic advancement. As the late president of Fisk University, Charles S. Johnson, put it: "We cannot escape the fact that the Negro minority market alone, even when held down by unequal opportunity and limited education to one half of its potential, is equal to the total [national income] of Canada or to our total foreign exports." [7]

Furthermore, as Dabbs so wisely observed, "As [the Negro] gains economic power, he moves toward equality in economic relations. He is already equal in a detail of our financial life: at the bank counter he is plain John Doe. He is rapidly becoming an equal in the world of merchandising: all folding money is green. As he gains the ballot, he will become a political equal. As he gains legal support, he moves toward equality in civil relations. . . . And now, as the Negro gains equality, he will tend to accept himself as an equal, and this will put added pressure on the white man to accept him. For to some degree we accept every man's evaluation of himself." [8]

Similarly, Key has pointed to important factors altering the central place of the Negro in Southern politics, including the heavy outmigration of Negroes from the plantation areas, the increasing organization of urban labor in the South, and the increasing fellow-feeling of Southern industrial and financial interests with northern Republicanism. He particularly emphasizes the effects of Negro migration to Southern cities, arguing that the movement of Southern Negroes to Houston, Atlanta, and Birmingham has somewhat the same political effect as their movement to points outside the South. It is true that the moderating and liberalizing influences of

Southern urbanization on race relations have been held in check by widespread gerrymandering against urban centers and by the dominance of the plantation counties in the conservative wing of the Southern Democratic party.[9] The thousands of low-income rural whites moving into Southern cities do not leave their race prejudices and hatreds behind. Even so, as ways are found for the Southern cities to throw off the tyrannical rule of rural minorities and as these cities accelerate their industrial development sufficiently to remove the feeling of economic insecurity among their vast new white wage-earning classes, a gradual improvement in urban race relations appears highly probable.

If they are left to their own resources and given that local autonomy without which the States' Rights doctrine is hypocritical and empty, the South's cities can ameliorate the race problem as its semifeudalistic rural areas as yet cannot. The differences between the South's primitive rural folk society and its modern industrial-urban society are profound. In the South's traditional folk society, laws do follow customs, whereas in the South's rapidly growing industrial society "custom is becoming less important and law more important." Increasingly, in Dabbs's words, "Daily, abstract justice is of more concern, concrete habits of less. The demand that the South change, perhaps rather sharply, its customs is simply the demand that it act in the fashion of the industrial society to which it aspires and which it is rapidly becoming." In the process of its industrial-urban development the South is at last learning "how men may live generously and easily without oppressing the laboring class; . . . indeed, [how] the entire society can advance only as all its members, its [white and Negro] laborers included, advance also." In advancing, the South is finally substituting an etiquette of equality for one of inequality.[10]

While the industrial-urban development of the South has already contributed much to removing the heavy load of history from its tired old back, the danger remains that more demagogues may yet have their day. If Southern political leadership allows the closing of its hard-won and priceless public-school systems, the breakdown of law and order and freedom of discussion, the continued virtual disenfranchisement of its more moderate and liberal urban sector, and the destruction of its rising state universities, Southern economic development for whites and Negroes alike can easily be set back by half a century. As the contrasting experiences of North Carolina and Arkansas make painfully clear, the directions set by state leadership are of paramount importance. How much better for the South if its social, economic, and political leaders would heed the voices of its great native sons of the past!

Thomas Jefferson wrote a friend in 1786: "Preach, my dear Sir, a crusade against ignorance; establish and improve the law for educating the common people. Let our countrymen know that . . . the tax which will be paid for this purpose, is not more than the thousandth part of what will be paid . . . if we leave the people in ignorance." A century later, unembittered by defeat, Robert E. Lee not only demanded "the thorough education of all classes of [Southern] people" but stated that the great aim of every Southerner should be to unite in "the allayment of passion, the dissipation of prejudice, and the restoration of reason." "Abandon all these local animosities," he exhorted, "and make your sons Americans." Woodrow Wilson wrote in a similar spirit: "Any man who revives the issue of sectionalism in this country, is unworthy of the government of the nation; he shows himself a provincial; he shows that he himself does not know the various sections of his own country; he shows that he has shut his heart up in a little province and that those who do not see the special interests of that province are to him sectional, while he alone is national. That is the depth of unpatriotic feeling." * Jefferson, Lee, Wilson—these are the great and immortal voices of that South which is eternally worth preserving! Judged

---

* Jefferson's letter of August 13, 1786, to George Wythe (*The Life and Selected Writings of Thomas Jefferson*, edited by Adrienne Koch and William Peden [New York, 1944], p. 395); Lee as quoted in Mims, *The Advancing South* (New York, 1926), pp. 4-5; Wilson as quoted in Odum, *Southern Regions*, p. 257. Wilson's criticism of provincialism, it should be noted, need not be limited to Southerners.

against such giants among men, the South's Tillmans, Bilbos, Faubuses, and Griffins are seen for the pygmies they really are.

Unless the South is again willing to secede from the Union—and no one really believes that it is—it is high time that the region faced up to its obligations as an integral part of the Union. Governor Leroy Collins of Florida clearly did so in a recent statement: "Talking . . . in terms of realities, we should recognize the United States Supreme Court decision can only be changed by the Court, itself, or by a constitutional amendment declaring racial segregation in public schools permissible. And no one seriously expects that either of these things will happen." [11] While Southerners have always had a "remarkable capacity for unreality," this reality they must somehow bring themselves to face and face squarely. This is admittedly asking a lot, for, as Louis D. Rubin, Jr., recently wrote in a somewhat different context, "Working against a successful outcome is that characteristic ingrained in Southern life . . .—the willingness to ignore practical problems requiring common effort, planning and foresight, in favor of a concentration on personal, inner satisfactions alone. The Southerner is . . . temperamentally opposed to the kind of necessarily abstract analysis that would permit him to work out a long range solution. . . . [Nonetheless, the South] must do what it has never done before—sit down and think out its course, prepare for the future without waiting until the next crisis is upon it." Such behavior is also most un-Southern, but the South must rise to the occasion.[12]

If the South could at last take such a fresh, honest, and hardheaded look at the race problem, the gains which would accrue to the region would extend far beyond matters of race. For race has so shackled the Southern mind that it has been incapable of accepting social responsibility for the general welfare or of organizing common efforts for common benefit in other important directions as well. There is indeed a danger that "in accepting the new, the urban, and the industrial," the South will wantonly discard the old, which "would quickly make the South a second-rate North at best, with all moorings gone." * With proper foresight and constructive planning, the South's industrial-urban development need not take such an unhappy turn. As Polk recently wrote, "the South is being industrialized at a time when industry has attained not only a new efficiency but a new sense of social responsibility, and when city planning is a technique by which cities, instead of degenerating into blighted areas and slums, can grow in convenience, comfort, and beauty as well as size." [13]

With effective and constructive leadership, it is wholly possible that "the last half of the twentieth century belongs to the South!" Unfortunately, an adequate supply of such leadership has not been forthcoming. The plain fact is that the Southern social and political structure has maintained the form, while losing the ameliorative socially responsible substance, of an aristocratic system. The South's privileged classes have largely abdicated their positions of leadership and have left the masses inadequately prepared educationally and economically to provide effective leadership of their own through more democratic channels.

While there is a great need for democratizing the Southern political structure, it is too slow a process to fill immediately the vacuum of leadership in these current troubled times. It is those Southern citizens who presently occupy high social, economic, and political positions who must fill the gap in the meantime. If they are to do so, they must relearn some of the long-forgotten aristocratic principles of the Old South at its best—"sacrifice and obligation and a concern for the welfare of others." [14] Or, in Dabbs's challenging words, "As leaders of society, they should be able to see that at long last their society is changing and that it's their job to lead it. The leaders of the Old South were not afraid to stand upon their own feet. The

* Ellington White, in Rubin and Kilpatrick, eds., *The Lasting South,* p. 162. Cf. Dabbs's similar good-humored warning (*Southern Heritage,* p. 179) that "Industrialism is the one abstraction we're buying now, lock, stock, and barrel. We'll have to be on our toes to keep it from making Yankees of us all."

leaders of the New might do well to be more truly traditional than they are." [15]

Thus far, I have directed my criticisms of a failure of constructive leadership against such broad and admittedly ill-defined groups as the South's "upper class," "privileged class," and so on. Even if they agree with me, most Southern economists probably do not identify themselves with such groups enough to have personal twinges of conscience about their own inadequate role in these important matters. Yet, as part of the South's small but growing intellectual elite, we Southern economists are members of the region's "privileged class" and opinion leadership—by training if not by wealth or family position. As such, have we not also shirked our own obligations as social scientists and citizens? Cash has observed that in Southern universities during the early part of the present century the field of economics advanced even more slowly than did the field of history. "Adam Smith still was generally presented as having the same absolute validity as Isaac Newton. And the teaching of [economics] was mainly in the hands of dull men who carefully avoided examining the current scene in the South itself." [16] Certainly, our profession in the South can no longer be charged with being outside of the mainstream of American (and Western) economic thought. But haven't we found it too easy to leave to our more courageous colleagues in sociology the analysis of the most important and controversial social issues of today, most of which have enormous economic implications?

I believe that we have. In his recent review of Becker's book, *The Economics of Discrimination*, Donald Dewey of Duke University was undoubtedly right in his melancholy observation that "apparently, economists in the South must still look to Chicago for pioneer work on the region's important problem." * While our principal professional obligation is sound and objective economic analysis of problems of regional economic development, among other things,

* *Southern Economic Journal*, XXIV (1958), 496. Professor Dewey has been virtually the only white economist in any Southern university to devote a substantial amount of research to the economic aspects of race.

such analyses can hardly be adequate or realistic if they ignore the direct economic effects of race and other noneconomic factors. Nor can we afford to hide such broader analyses, once made, under a bushel simply because life will be more comfortable if we do. While, as economists, we cannot say that the South should choose progress over tradition, I believe that we have a firm obligation to use our analytical tools to make clear to the Southern public the inconsistencies in trying to achieve both objectives at once.*

What I have said of the obligations of the Southern economist apply with almost equal force to other Southern social scientists and university professors, not to mention the important business and professional leaders who are the products of Southern university education. Collectively, we are the South's intellectual aristocracy, or the South has none. Furthermore, quite apart from our professional or leadership obligations we of this intellectual aristocracy have vital duties to perform as enlightened citizens and as men of flesh-and-blood and moral convictions. Whether native sons or ex-Yankees, we are now Southerners by choice rather than necessity. There is something pleasant and precious about the Southern way of life which we like, or we wouldn't be here. But like all ways of life, the Southern way is not perfect. If, against one of the South's least fortunate traditions, we are permitted to express even unpopular ideas freely and can feel hope for the South's economic future, most of us want to stay. But if we do, it will be because, in Walter Hines Page's striking phrase, "We look forward to a golden age that we may surely help to bring, not back to one that never was."

* Professor Lorin A. Thompson of the University of Virginia deserves a favorable citation here. His recent economic analysis of Virginia's public-school crisis was not only comprehensive and sound but was courageous and influential as well.

Notes

NOTES

CHAPTER 1

1. Quoted in Howard W. Odum, *Southern Regions of the United States* (Chapel Hill, 1936), p. 531.
2. Edwin Mims, *The Advancing South* (New York, 1926), pp. 24, vii.
3. Twelve Southerners, *I'll Take My Stand* (New York, 1930), pp. 69, 52, 12, 15.
4. *Ibid.*, pp. xix, xx.
5. Mims, *Advancing South*, pp. vii, 9. Cf. Odum, *Southern Regions*, pp. 211-13.
6. Harry S. Ashmore, *An Epitaph for Dixie* (New York, 1957), p. 45.
7. Louis D. Rubin Jr., and James Jackson Kilpatrick, editors, *The Lasting South* (Chicago, 1957), p. 15; cf. Walter Sullivan (*ibid.*, pp. 118-19), Ronald F. Howell (*ibid.*, pp. 161-62), and James Jackson Kilpatrick (*ibid.*, pp. 192-93). On the other side, cf. the similar views of Odum (*Southern Regions*, pp. 22, 55-57, 225-29), W. J. Cash (*The Mind of the South* [New York, 1956], pp. 197-99, 243-45, 383), and James McBride Dabbs (*The Southern Heritage* [New York, 1958], pp. 169 ff.).
8. These conclusions are partly based on the findings of a large-scale research project which has been under way at Vanderbilt University since 1952. See, for example, Anthony M. Tang, *Economic Development in the Southern Piedmont 1860-1950: Its Impact on Agriculture* (Chapel Hill, 1958); and my own recent publications, including the following: "Some Foundations of Economic Development in the Upper East Tennessee Valley, 1850-1900," *Journal of Political Economy*, LXIV (1956), 277-302, 400-15; "The Effects of Industrial Development on Tennessee Valley Agriculture, 1900-1950," *Journal of Farm Economics*, XXXVIII (1956), 1636-49; and "Human Resources and Industrial Development in the Upper East Tennessee Valley, 1900-1950," *Quarterly Journal of Economics*, LXXI (1957), 289-316.

Notes

CHAPTER 2

1. Paul H. Johnstone, "Old Ideals versus New Ideas in Farm Life," in *Farmers in a Changing World* [Yearbook of Agriculture 1940], (Washington), pp. 116-17, 114.

2. Johnstone, *ibid.*, pp. 124-27; and Everett E. Edwards, "American Agriculture—the First 300 Years," *ibid.*, pp. 209-10.

3. Dabbs, *Southern Heritage*, pp. 173-75.

4. Nicholls, "Some Foundations of Economic Development in the Upper East Tennessee Valley, 1850-1900," especially pp. 413-14. Cf. Constantine G. Belissary's excellent unpublished doctoral dissertation, "The Rise of the Industrial Spirit in Tennessee, 1865-1885" (Vanderbilt University, 1949).

5. C. Vann Woodward, *Origins of the New South 1877-1913* (Baton Rouge, La., 1951), pp. 152, 19, 21, 158, 154-55.

6. *Ibid.*, pp. 222-25; and Cash, *Mind of the South*, pp. 206-7.

7. Quoted in Belissary, "Rise of the Industrial Spirit in Tennessee," pp. 246, 85.

8. Woodward, *Origins of the New South*, pp. 58-59, 65.

9. Twelve Southerners, *I'll Take My Stand*, pp. x-xi.

10. *Ibid.*, pp. xi-xviii.

11. *Ibid.*, pp. xvii, xix; and Johnstone, "Old Ideals versus New Ideas in Farm Life," p. 117.

12. Twelve Southerners, *I'll Take My Stand*, pp. 216, 12.

13. Herbert Agar and Allen Tate, editors, *Who Owns America?* (New York, 1936), pp. 117-21, 131-34.

14. *Ibid.*, pp. 162-63.

15. *Ibid.*, pp. 164-65, 168, 177.

16. Dabbs, *Southern Heritage*, pp. 133-35, 140-42.

17. William T. Polk, *Southern Accent: From Uncle Remus to Oak Ridge* (New York, 1953), p. 243.

18. Twelve Southerners, *I'll Take My Stand*, p. xix.

19. Rubin and Kilpatrick, eds., *The Lasting South*, pp. 148-49.

20. Quoted in Mims, *Advancing South*, pp. 44, 78.

21. See, for example, Stefan H. Robock and John M. Peterson, "Fact and Fiction About Southern Labor," *Harvard Business Review* (March-April, 1954). For a comparable study of the favorable experience with Southern farm migrants in Northern industry, see D. Gale Johnson, "Comparability of Labor Capacities of Farm and Non-Farm Labor," *American Economic Review*, XLIII (1953), 296-313.

22. Joseph S. Davis, "Agricultural Fundamentalism," in Norman E. Himes, editor, *Economics, Sociology, and the Modern World* (Cambridge, Mass., 1935), p. 21. The entire essay is highly recommended in the present context.

CHAPTER 3

1. Paul Cohen-Portheim, *England, the Unknown Isle*, translated by Alan Harris (London, 1930), pp. 117, 69, 107-8, 46.
2. *Ibid.*, pp. 107-8, 69-70, 37, 226.
3. Cf. Nicholls, "Accommodating Economic Change in Underdeveloped Countries," pp. 160-61, 164-65.
4. Cf. Nicholls, "Some Foundations of Economic Development," pp. 403-5; and L. C. Gray, *History of Agriculture in the Southern United States to 1860* (Washington, 1933), I, 442, 487-90.
5. Twelve Southerners, *I'll Take My Stand*, p. 12.
6. Ashmore, *Epitaph for Dixie*, p. 19.
7. Rubin and Kilpatrick, eds., *The Lasting South*, p. 147.
8. Cash, *Mind of the South*, pp. 71-73, 84.
9. *Ibid.*, p. 89.
10. *Ibid.*, pp. 98-99, 94.
11. *Ibid.*, pp. 171-75, 179.
12. Rubin and Kilpatrick, eds., *The Lasting South*, pp. 174-75.
13. Woodward, *Origins of the New South*, pp. 150-52, 371, 477.
14. *Ibid.*, pp. 140-41, commenting upon Broadus Mitchell and George S. Mitchell, *The Industrial Revolution in the South* (Baltimore, 1930), pp. 294, 106-7.
15. Odum, *Southern Regions*, pp. 57-59.
16. Polk, *Southern Accent*, p. 245.
17. Rubin and Kilpatrick, eds., *The Lasting South*, p. 123; and Dabbs, *Southern Heritage*, pp. 183-84.
18. Rubin and Kilpatrick, eds., *The Lasting South*, p. 170.
19. Twelve Southerners, *I'll Take My Stand*, pp. xviii, 119; Odum, *Southern Regions*, p. 213.
20. Quoted in Mims, *Advancing South*, p. 78.
21. Dabbs, *Southern Heritage*, pp. 112-13.
22. V. O. Key, Jr., *Southern Politics in State and Nation* (New York, 1949), pp. 19-20, 183-84.

Notes

CHAPTER 4

1. Cf., for example, S. J. Folmsbee, *Sectionalism and Internal Improvements in Tennessee, 1796-1845*, East Tennessee Historical Society (Knoxville, 1939); Charles H. Ambler, *Sectionalism in Virginia from 1776 to 1861* (Chicago, 1910); and Woodward, *Origins of the New South*, pp. 327-28.

2. Woodward, *Origins of the New South*, p. 19; cf. Key, *Southern Politics*, p. 6.

3. Woodward, *Origins of the New South*, pp. 20-21, 328, 28-30.

4. *Ibid.*, pp. 51, 321, 211, 221, 249-51; and Key, *Southern Politics*, p. 665.

5. Rubin and Kilpatrick, eds., *The Lasting South*, p. 122.

6. Woodward, *Origins of the New South*, pp. 246, 249, 321-22; Key, *Southern Politics*, pp. 6-9.

7. Woodward, *Origins of the New South*, pp. 350, 353.

8. *Ibid.*, pp. 329, 340-41, 330, 336-37.

9. *Ibid.*, pp. 341-42, 331-37.

10. Key, *Southern Politics*, p. 8; cf. pp. 665-67.

11. *Ibid.*, pp. 504-5.

12. *Ibid.*, pp. 506-8, 523.

13. *Ibid.*, pp. 514-17, 526-28; and Cortez A. M. Ewing and James E. Titus in Rupert B. Vance and Nicholas J. Demerath, editors, *The Urban South* (Chapel Hill, 1954), p. 239.

14. Woodward, *Origins of the New South*, Chapter XIV, especially pp. 371-73, 477.

15. Ashmore, *Epitaph for Dixie*, p. 111.

16. Vance and Demerath, eds., *Urban South*, pp. 235, 232; and Ashmore, *Epitaph for Dixie*, pp. 110-11.

17. Dabbs, *Southern Heritage*, pp. 115-16.

18. Ashmore, *Epitaph for Dixie*, p. 35.

19. Dabbs, *Southern Heritage*, pp. 111-12.

20. Key, *Southern Politics*, p. 671.

21. Nicholls, "Accommodating Economic Change in Underdeveloped Countries," pp. 162-64.

22. Wilma Dykeman and James Stokely, *Neither Black nor White* (New York, 1957), p. 110.

23. Ashmore, *Epitaph for Dixie*, p. 38.

24. Odum, *Southern Regions*, p. 259.

25. Nicholls, "Accommodating Economic Change in Underdeveloped Countries," pp. 164-66.

Notes

26. Rubin and Kilpatrick, eds., *The Lasting South*, p. 175 (Hazel); and Odum, *Southern Regions*, p. 531 (Mumford).
27. G. Lowes Dickinson, *The Greek View of Life* (22nd edition; London, 1949), pp. 134-35.
28. G. Lowes Dickinson, *The Choice Before Us* (London, 1917), Chapter XII.

CHAPTER 5

1. Cash, *Mind of the South*, pp. 88-89.
2. *Ibid.*, p. 163.
3. A. C. Pigou, *The Economics of Welfare* (London, 1948), pp. 118, 119-22.
4. Ambler, *Sectionalism in Virginia*, pp. 273-78, 281-82; and Albert Ogden Porter, *County Government in Virginia: A Legislative History, 1607-1904* (New York, 1947), pp. 240-41.
5. Philip M. Hamer, editor, *Tennessee: A History, 1673-1932*, American Historical Society (New York, 1933), pp. 257-58, 353-59; and Thomas P. Abernethy, *From Frontier to Plantation in Tennessee* (Chapel Hill, 1932), pp. 261, 360.
6. Hamilton J. Eckenrode, *The Political History of Virginia during the Reconstruction* (Baltimore, 1904), pp. 20-24, 52, 87, 93-94; William C. Pendleton, *Political History of Appalachian Virginia, 1776-1927* (Dayton, Va., 1927), p. 283; Porter, *County Government in Virginia*, pp. 259-60, 291-93, 296-97; and Matthew Page Andrews, *Virginia: The Old Dominion* (New York, 1937), pp. 564-66.
7. Robert H. White, *Development of the Tennessee State Educational Organization, 1796-1929* (Kingsport, Tenn., 1929), Chapter IV and pp. 140-41; Belissary, "Industrial Spirit in Tennessee," pp. 11-13, 237-48; and T. R. Snavely *et al.*, *State Grants-in-Aid in Virginia* (New York, 1933), p. 55.
8. Mims, *Advancing South*, pp. 4-5, 32, 78, 20.
9. Woodward, *Origins of the New South*, pp. 396-406.
10. Twelve Southerners, *I'll Take My Stand*, pp. 114-15, 118-20.
11. Cf. Dykeman and Stokely, *Neither Black nor White*, pp. 172-73.
12. Dabbs, *Southern Heritage*, p. 176.
13. Associated Press, "Atlanta Nears the Hour of Decision," *Nashville Tennessean* (January 11, 1959), p. 3-B.
14. Address of March 15, 1959, at Thomas Jefferson High School, Richmond, Va.

15. Address of April 6, 1959, before the Rockingham, Va., Development Corporation.
16. Two feature news stories on Little Rock by Garry Fullerton, *Nashville Tennessean* (May 31 and June 1, 1959).
17. *Ibid.; Time* (May 4, 1959), p. 17; Ralph McGill, column in *Nashville Tennessean* (March 10, 1959), p. 10.
18. Fullerton, *Nashville Tennessean* (June 1, 1959).
19. From an advertisement published nationally by the state of Mississippi.
20. *New South* (May, 1956), p. 15, quoting Opie L. Shelton.
21. Sylvia Porter, column in *Raleigh News and Observer* (March 25, 1956); Gainsbrough in *Atlanta Constitution* (February 27, 1959); Boyd Campbell of Jackson, Miss., in an address before the Southern States Industrial Relations Conference at Birmingham in early 1956; Ivan Allen, Jr., of Atlanta in *Atlanta Journal* (December 10, 1958); "Segregation Drying Up Sources of Funds for Southern Schools," *St. Louis Post-Dispatch* (September 21, 1958).
22. Ashmore, *Epitaph for Dixie*, pp. 118, 120; cf. p. 148.
23. *New South* (January, 1959), p. 15.
24. Malcolm Seawell, "North Carolina at Crossroad," *ibid.*, pp. 3-5.
25. Quoted in Ashmore, *Epitaph for Dixie*, p. 171.
26. Compiled or computed from Everett S. Lee *et al.*, *Population Redistribution and Economic Growth*, Vol. I (American Philosophical Society, *Memoirs*, XLV [Philadelphia, 1957]), passim.
27. *Ibid.*
28. Dykeman and Stokely, *Neither Black nor White*, pp. 123, 325.
29. *Ibid.*, p. 124.
30. Dabbs, *Southern Heritage*, p. 154.

CHAPTER 6

1. Avery Craven, *Democracy in American Life* (Chicago, 1941), pp. 46-47, 50-51.
2. Odum, *Southern Regions*, pp. 13, 211-13.
3. Cash, *Mind of the South*, pp. 99-101, 144-46, 150.
4. Glasgow quoted in Dykeman and Stokely, *Neither Black nor White*, p. 347; Dabbs, *Southern Heritage*, p. 147; Woodward, *Origins of the New South*, p. 158.
5. T. V. Smith, "Justice Holmes: Voice of Democratic Evolution," in Charner M. Perry, editor, *The Philosophy of American Democracy* (Chicago, 1943), pp. 119, 141.

6. *Ibid.*, pp. 138-39, 125.

7. Dabbs, *Southern Heritage*, p. 148.

8. Dykeman and Stokely, *Neither Black nor White*, p. 166.

9. Cash, *Mind of the South*, p. 56.

10. Hodding Carter, *The Angry Scar: The Story of Reconstruction* (New York, 1959), p. 387; and Dykeman and Stokely, *Neither Black nor White*, p. 16.

11. Associated Press, *Nashville Tennessean* (May 23, 1959), p. 1.

12. Rubin and Kilpatrick, eds., *The Lasting South*, pp. 148-49, 145.

13. *Ibid.*, p. 151; and Cash, *Mind of the South*, p. 320.

14. Rubin and Kilpatrick, eds., *The Lasting South*, pp. 152-53.

15. Dabbs, *Southern Heritage*, pp. 170-72, 176, 178-79.

16. *Ibid.*, p. 174.

17. Quoted in Mims, *Advancing South*, p. 158.

18. Cash, *Mind of the South*, p. 328; cf. *ibid.*, pp. 321-27, and Woodward, *Origins of the New South*, pp. 440-46.

19. Ashmore, *Epitaph for Dixie*, pp. 155-56, 158.

20. Dykeman and Stokely, *Neither Black nor White*, p. 191.

21. *AAUP Bulletin*, XLIV (Spring, 1958), 158-61, 164, 168.

22. *Ibid.*, p. 161n.

23. Dr. F. Douglas Lawrason, provost for medical affairs, in the *Arkansas Gazette* (January 16, 1959).

24. O. B. Newton, Jr., vice-president and sales manager, C. B. Fleet Company, in testimony before House Privileges and Elections Committee, April 17, 1959.

25. James Montgomery, series of articles, "How Could Shut Schools Affect State Economy," *Atlanta Constitution* (November 30–December 4, 1958).

26. "Georgians Resist Closed Schools," *New South* (April, 1959), pp. 4-5.

27. Calvin B. Hoover and B. U. Ratchford, *Economic Resources and Policies of the South* (New York, 1951), pp. 38-42.

CHAPTER 7

1. Quoted in Dykeman and Stokely, *Neither Black nor White*, p. 322.

2. Quoted *ibid.*, pp. 332-33.

3. For detailed statistics, see *Farm Population*, August, 1956, Series Census-AMS (P-27), No. 22 (Washington, 1956), especially Table F, p. 8.

4. *Virginia Quarterly Review,* XXXI (1955), 222.

5. Key, *Southern Politics,* p. 675.

6. The data which follow were compiled from either census reports or Hoover and Ratchford, *Economic Resources.*

7. Quoted in Dykeman and Stokely, *Neither Black nor White,* p. 325.

8. Dabbs, *Southern Heritage,* pp. 163-64.

9. Key, *Southern Politics,* pp. 669-70, 672-74.

10. Dabbs, *Southern Heritage,* pp. 162-63, 179.

11. Quoted in *New South* (December, 1958), p. 15.

12. Rubin and Kilpatrick, eds., *The Lasting South,* p. 15.

13. Polk, *Southern Accent,* p. 253.

14. Robert Hazel in Rubin and Kilpatrick, eds., *The Lasting South,* p. 170.

15. Dabbs, *Southern Heritage,* pp. 119-20.

16. Cash, *Mind of the South,* p. 323.

Bibliography

BIBLIOGRAPHY

ABERNETHY, THOMAS P. *From Frontier to Plantation in Tennessee* (Chapel Hill: University of North Carolina Press, 1932).

AGAR, HERBERT, and ALLEN TATE, editors. *Who Owns America?* (Boston and New York: Houghton Mifflin Company, 1936).

AMBLER, CHARLES H. *Sectionalism in Virginia from 1776 to 1861* (Chicago: University of Chicago Press, 1910).

ANDREWS, MATTHEW PAGE. *Virginia, The Old Dominion* (New York: Doubleday, Doran & Co., 1937).

ASHMORE, HARRY S. *An Epitaph for Dixie* (New York: W. W. Norton & Co., 1957, 1958).

BECKER, GARY S. *The Economics of Discrimination* (Chicago: University of Chicago Press, 1957).

BELISSARY, CONSTANTINE. "The Rise of the Industrial Spirit in Tennessee, 1865-1885," unpublished doctoral dissertation, Vanderbilt University, 1949.

CARTER, HODDING. *The Angry Scar: The Story of Reconstruction* (Garden City, New York: Doubleday and Company, 1959).

CASH, W. J. *The Mind of the South* (Garden City, New York: Doubleday Anchor Books, Doubleday & Co., 1956).

COHEN-PORTHEIM, PAUL. *England, the Unknown Isle*, translated by Alan Harris (London: Duckworth, 1930).

CRAVEN, AVERY. *Democracy in American Life* (Chicago: University of Chicago Press, 1941).

DABBS, JAMES McBRIDE. *The Southern Heritage* (New York: Alfred A. Knopf, Inc., 1958).

DANIELS, JONATHAN. "Men at a Corner," *Virginia Quarterly Review*, XXXI, No. 2 (Spring, 1955), 213-22.

DAVIS, JOSEPH S. "Agricultural Fundamentalism," in Norman E. Himes, editor, *Economics, Sociology, and the Modern World* (Cambridge: Harvard University Press, 1935), pp. 3-22.

Bibliography

DICKINSON, G. LOWES. *The Choice Before Us* (London: G. Allen & Unwin, Ltd., 1917).

———. *The Greek View of Life* (22nd edition; London: Methuen & Co., Ltd., 1949).

DYKEMAN, WILMA, and JAMES STOKELY. *Neither Black nor White* (New York and Toronto: Rinehart & Company, 1957).

ECKENRODE, HAMILTON J. *The Political History of Virginia during the Reconstruction* (Baltimore: The Johns Hopkins Press, 1904).

EDWARDS, EVERETT E. "American Agriculture—the First 300 Years," *Farmers in a Changing World*, Yearbook of Agriculture 1940 (Washington: U.S. Department of Agriculture, 1940), 171-266.

Farm Population, August, 1956, Series Census-AMS (P-27), No. 22 (Washington, 1956).

FOLMSBEE, S. J. *Sectionalism and Internal Improvements in Tennessee, 1796-1845* (Knoxville: East Tennessee Historical Society, 1939).

GRAY, L. C. *History of Agriculture in the Southern United States to 1860* (Washington: Carnegie Institute, 1933), Vols. I and II.

HAMER, PHILIP M., editor. *Tennessee: A History, 1673-1932* (4 vols.; New York: American Historical Society, 1933).

HARDIN, CHARLES M. "The Bureau of Agricultural Economics Under Fire: A Study in Valuation Conflicts," *Journal of Farm Economics*, XXVIII (1946), 635-68.

HOOVER, CALVIN B., and B. U. RATCHFORD. *Economic Resources and Policies of the South* (New York: The Macmillan Company, 1951).

JENKINS, IREDELL. "Segregation and the Professor," *AAUP Bulletin*, XLIII (1957), 10-18.

JOHNSON, D. GALE. "Comparability of Labor Capacities of Farm and Non-Farm Labor," *American Economic Review*, XLIII (1953), 296-313.

JOHNSTONE, PAUL H. "Old Ideals versus New Ideas in Farm Life," in *Farmers in a Changing World*, Yearbook of Agriculture 1940 (Washington: U.S. Department of Agriculture, 1940), 111-67.

KEY, V. O., JR. *Southern Politics in State and Nation* (New York: Alfred A. Knopf, Inc., 1949).

KOCH, ADRIENNE, and WILLIAM PEDEN, editors. *The Life and Selected Writings of Thomas Jefferson* (New York: Random House, Modern Library Edition, 1944).

Bibliography

LEE, EVERETT S., *et al. Population Redistribution and Economic Growth, U.S. 1870-1950*, Vol. I (American Philosophical Society, *Memoirs*, XLV [Philadelphia, 1957]).

McELVEEN, JACKSON V., and KENNETH L. BACHMAN. *Low Production Farms*, Agri. Info. Bulletin 108 (Washington: U.S. Department of Agriculture, 1953).

MANTOUX, PAUL. *The Industrial Revolution in the Eighteenth Century* (New York: The Macmillan Company, 1927).

MIMS, EDWIN. *The Advancing South* (Garden City: Doubleday, Page, & Company, 1926).

MITCHELL, BROADUS, and GEORGE S. MITCHELL. *The Industrial Revolution in the South* (Baltimore: The Johns Hopkins Press; London: H. Milford, Oxford University Press, 1930).

NICHOLLS, WILLIAM H. "The Effects of Industrial Development on Tennessee Valley Agriculture, 1900-1950," *Journal of Farm Economics*, XXXVIII (1956), 1636-49.

———. "Human Resources and Industrial Development in the Upper East Tennessee Valley, 1900-1950," *Quarterly Journal of Economics*, LXXI (1957), 289-316.

———. "Multiple-Unit Operations and Gross Farm Income Distribution within the Old Cotton Belt," *Southern Economic Journal*, XIX(1953), 467-80.

———. "Some Foundations of Economic Development in the Upper East Tennessee Valley, 1850-1900," *Journal of Political Economy*, LXIV (1956), 277-302, 400-415.

———. "Accommodating Economic Change in Underdeveloped Countries," *American Economic Review* (Proceedings), XLIX (May, 1959), 156-68.

ODUM, HOWARD W. *Southern Regions of the United States* (Chapel Hill: University of North Carolina Press, 1936).

PENDLETON, WILLIAM C. *Political History of Appalachian Virginia, 1776-1927* (Dayton, Va.: Shenandoah Press, 1927).

PERRY, CHARNER M., ed. *The Philosophy of Democracy* (Chicago: University of Chicago Press, 1943).

PIGOU, A. C. *The Economics of Welfare* (London: Macmillan & Company, Ltd.; New York: St. Martin's Press, Inc., 1948).

POLK, WILLIAM T. *Southern Accent: From Uncle Remus to Oak Ridge* (New York: William Morrow and Company, 1953).

Bibliography

PORTER, ALBERT OGDEN. *County Government in Virginia: A Legislative History, 1607-1904* (New York: Columbia University Press, 1947).

ROBOCK, STEFAN H., and JOHN M. PETERSON. "Fact and Fiction About Southern Labor," *Harvard Business Review*, XXXII (March-April, 1954), pp. 79-88.

RUBIN, LOUIS D., JR., and JAMES JACKSON KILPATRICK, editors. *The Lasting South: Fourteen Southerners Look at Their Home* (Chicago: Henry Regnery Company, 1957).

SMITH, T. V. "Justice Holmes: Voice of Democratic Evolution," in Charner M. Perry, editor, *The Philosophy of American Democracy* (Chicago: University of Chicago Press, 1943), 119-152.

SNAVELY, T. R., *et al. State Grants-in-Aid in Virginia* (New York: Century Co., 1933).

TANG, ANTHONY M. *Economic Development in the Southern Piedmont 1860-1950: Its Impact on Agriculture* (Chapel Hill: University of North Carolina Press, 1958).

TWELVE SOUTHERNERS. *I'll Take My Stand: The South and the Agrarian Tradition* (New York and London: Harper & Brothers, 1930).

THOMPSON, LORIN A. "Some Economic Aspects of Virginia's Current Educational Crisis" (Charlottesville, Va., undated) (processed).

VANCE, RUPERT B., and NICHOLAS J. DEMERATH, editors. *The Urban South* (Chapel Hill: University of North Carolina Press, 1954).

WHITE, ROBERT H. *Development of the Tennessee State Educational Organization, 1796-1929* (Kingsport, Tenn.: Southern Publishers, 1929).

WOODWARD, C. VANN. *Origins of the New South 1877-1913* (Baton Rouge: Louisiana State University Press, 1951). Vol. IX of Wendell Holmes Stephenson and E. Merton Coulter, editors, *A History of the South.*